The Dialogue between Higher Education Research and Practice

The Dialogue between Higher Education Research and Practice

25 Years of EAIR

Edited by

Roddy Begg

KLUWER ACADEMIC PUBLISHERS

DORDRECHT / BOSTON / LONDON

Library of Congress Cataloging-in-Publication Data

ISBN 1-4020-1505-4

Published by Kluwer Academic Publishers,
P.O. Box 17, 3300 AA Dordrecht, The Netherlands.

Sold and distributed in North, Central and South America
by Kluwer Academic Publishers,
101 Philip Drive, Norwell, MA 02061, U.S.A.

In all other countries, sold and distributed
by Kluwer Academic Publishers,
P.O. Box 322, 3300 AH Dordrecht, The Netherlands.

Printed on acid-free paper

Printed in the Netherlands.

TABLE OF CONTENTS

NOTES ON CONTRIBUTORS

BERIT ASKLING is Professor in Education at the Department of Education and Didactics of Goteborg University, Sweden. She is also Secretary General at the Committee of Educational Research at the Swedish Research Council and was formerly Vice Rector for quality affairs and former Dean of the School of Education. Her research field is 'Higher Education', in particular such themes as 'Impacts of reforms'. 'The changing university', 'The academic profession: evolving roles in diverse contexts' and 'Institutional governance'.

RODDY BEGG is Emeritus Secretary to the University of Aberdeen, Scotland. He served on the Executive Committee of EAIR for nine years (1993-2001), latterly as Secretary (1997-99), Vice-Chairman (1999-200) and Chairman (2000-01). He has been Editor (now Editor-in-Chief) of the Association's journal, Tertiary Education and Management (TEAM) since its establishment in 1994. He was co-founder and first Chairman of the Heads of Management and Administration Network in Europe (HUMANE) and a board member of the European Centre for the Strategic Management of Universities (ESMU). In retirement he is undertaking a little (gentle) consultancy for international bodies such as OECD.

After many years in university administration as Director of Institutional Research, Vice-President Academic and President, **CHARLES BELANGER** now shares his professional time between teaching management and consulting in developing countries. He served as President of the Canadian Society for the Study of Higher Education and Editor-in-chief of the Canadian Journal of Higher Education for almost a decade. As an AIR Board member, he led the fortunes of the 'European wing' from 1979 to 1982 before receiving the AIR Distinguished Member Award.

LEE HARVEY is Director of the Centre for Research and Evaluation at Sheffield Hallam University, UK. He has wide experience of social research, is published widely and is the Editor of Quality in Higher Education. He is Deputy Director of the Enhancing Student Employability Co-ordination team (ESECT), Vice-Chair of EAIR, a member of the Council of SRHE and an ex officio member of the Board of INQAAHE. He has also been a quality advisor to universities around the world and a keynote speaker at many major international conferences.

JEROEN HUISMAN is Research Co-ordinator in the Center for Higher Education Policy Studies, University of Twente, the Netherlands. His main research interests are in organisational change in higher education, and the impact of governmental policies on higher education. He is also editor of the journals TEAM and Perspectives. In the past decade he has been involved in research and consultancy projects for the Dutch Ministry of Education, Culture and Sciences, as well as for (inter)national organisations such as the EU.

FRANS KAISER is Research Associate and Co-ordinator of the Higher Education Monitor in the Center for Higher Education Policy Studies, University of Twente, the Netherlands. His main research interests are in comparative methodology, the use of indicators in higher education and research and systems approaches to higher education. In the past decade he has been involved in research projects for the Dutch Ministry of Education, Culture and Sciences and other ministries, as well as for (inter)national organisations such as the EU.

BARBARA M. KEHM is a senior researcher and research coordinator at the Institute for Higher Education Research in Wittenberg, Germany (HoF Wittenberg). Her field of specialisation is internationalisation of higher education and its effects on governance. She has been a member of the EAIR Executive Committee since 1998 and its Secretary since 1999. She is also member of the Editorial (Advisory) Boards of several journals, among them "Higher Education", and is an Editor of TEAM. During the last decade, she has conducted numerous research projects funded by the German Government and other national authorities and NGOs, as well as by a variety of supra-national organisations (EU, CRE/EUA, OECD etc.).

PETER MAASSEN is senior fellow at the Center for Higher Education Policy Studies (CHEPS), University of Twente, the Netherlands. At the University of Oslo he is the director of Hedda, a consortium of European centres on higher education research. He specialises in the public governance of higher education. In 1998 he was awarded a fellowship by the Society for Research on Higher Education (SRHE).

JOSE-GINES MORA is Professor in the Technical University of Valencia, Spain and Coordinator of the Accreditation Programme in the National Agency for Quality Assessment and Accreditation. His research is focused on Economics of Education and Higher Education. He has been member of the Executive Committee of EAIR for six years.

GUY NEAVE is Director of Research at the International Association of Universities, Paris, France and Professor of Comparative Education Policy Studies and Scientific Director at the Centre for Higher Education Policy Studies, Twente University, the Netherlands. An historian by formal training, he is Foreign Member of the National Academy of Education of the United States of America and Editor of the Quarterly Journal Higher Education Policy. Other activities keep him out of mischief, prime among which being the current President of EAIR.

MARVIN W. PETERSON is Professor of Higher Education and former Director of the Center for the Study of Higher Education at the University of Michigan and director of the Student Assessment Research Program of the National Center for Postsecondary Improvement. He is past president of the Association for the Study of Higher Education, the Association of Institutional Research and the Society for College and University Planning. His research and publications focus on organisational behaviour, governance, planning and management in higher education. He holds a BSc in Engineering and Mathemetics from Trinity College in Connecticut, an MBA from the Harvard Graduate School of Business Administration and a PhD in Higher Education and Organizational Psychology from the University of Michigan.

MICHAEL SHATTOCK is Visiting Professor of Higher Education and Joint Director of the MBA programme in Higher Education Management at the Institute of

Education, University of London. He was formerly Registrar of the University of Warwick. His most recent books are The UGC and the Management of British Universities (Open University Press) and The Creation of a University System (Blackwells) and his next book Managing Successful Universities (Open University Press) is due in October 2003. He is Editor of the journal "Higher Education Management and Policy" published by OECD.

BARBARA SPORN is Associate Professor at the Vienna University of Economics and Business Administration in Austria. In March 2002, she was elected Vice-Rector for International Relations at the same institution. She was Acting Assistant Professor at the School of Education and Research Fellow at the National Center for Postsecondary Improvement at Stanford University in 1996/97. Her empirical work is based on extensive field studies in the United States and Europe. She was a visiting scholar at New York University, the University of Michigan, and the University of California at Berkley. Her publications focus on environmental forces and organisational responses shaping higher education systems. Her recent work concentrates on international and comparative aspects of institutonal adaptation to changing environments at universities.

BJØRN STENSAKER is senior researcher at the Norwegian Institute for Studies in Research and Higher Education (NIFU) in Oslo, Norway. He is a political scientist by training, with research interests covering the areas of quality improvement, national evaluation and accreditation systems, ICT, and organisation and leadership in higher education. He is currently one of the Editors of TEAM, the journal of EAIR.

ULRICH TEICHLER is Professor at the University of Kassel, Germany and Director of the Centre for Research on Higher Education and Work. He was chairman of the Consortium of Higher Education Researchers (1988-89, 1992-98) and President of EAIR (1997-2001). Many of his about 800 publications focus on higher education and the world of work, higher education systems in comparative perspective and international cooperation and mobility.

LUIS E. VILA, Doctor in Economics, served as a Visiting Scholar to CERAS (Stanford University) in 1996. Currently, he is a full-time researcher and teacher at the University of Valencia, Spain. His research interests focus on the socio-economic effects of educational investment both at micro and macro levels. Main publications include papers on the estimation of rates of return to education, labour market effects of educational expansion, and non-monetary outcomes of education. Recent research focuses on the influence of education on job satisfaction. He also teaches Economics of Education both at undergraduate and graduate levels.

PART 1

HISTORY

GUY NEAVE

INSTITUTIONAL RESEARCH:

FROM CASE STUDY TO STRATEGIC INSTRUMENT

Abstract. This chapter traces the origins of Institutional Research from its beginnings in the US. Subsequently, it follows the development of the field in the UK and Sweden during the mid to late 1960s and, examining a rather different situation in France and Spain a quarter of a century later, analyses the factors and policies at the macro level that shaped the fortunes of Institutional Research. It provides some explanations for the apparent delay in the emergence of IR in the latter two countries. It concludes that competition, regionalisation and the managerial revolution are powerful influences in determining the spreading fortunes of our field.

INTRODUCTION

For a quarter of a century, the European Association for Institutional Research has brought together scholars and analysts, researchers and administrators. And, despite our title, from the very first, our community has never been confined simply to Europe. Quite on the contrary, it is a matter of record that we are part of a far wider constituency and, moreover one that, to judge by the numbers drawn in by recent conferences, is growing by leaps and bounds. Still, it is not out of place to admit that the origins of our particular Republic are not wholly of our own making. They reflect rather the projection into a European setting of a particular operational perspective on research into higher education the roots of which developed first on the Western side of the Atlantic.

What I want to do in this short excursion is to reflect a little on the origins of institutional research and the developmental trajectory that it has followed in Western Europe.

In many respects, a very good case can be made for arguing that institutional research is amongst the earliest modes to be employed in telling the story of higher learning. Certainly, it would not have passed under this rubric at the time when the earliest histories of individual universities - usually ancient - and within them the individual colleges – usually distinguished - were first penned. But if none would then have seen the saga in terms of being 'an institutional saga', it cannot be denied that their focus was most explicitly on what today's jargon would call the 'institutional level'.

Agreed, the present-day scope of institutional research has evolved far beyond the institutional history of higher education. Our field obeys the inexorable process of fragmentation, splitting off and re-coalescence, that process which Walter Metzger termed 'subject parturition' (Metzger 1987) and which remains a fundamental characteristic of knowledge in a dynamic state. Today, this dynamic has brought us to a condition, however, where a mort of difference exists between research at the institutional level and institutional research. To my way of looking at matters, the essential difference is less in methodology, technique and disciplinary related perspectives so much as the ultimate purpose on which they are brought to bear. What distinguishes institutional research stricto sensu is its application to the individual

3

establishment of higher education. It is in essence the institution interrogating itself to provide intelligence to its leadership on current performance the better to enable the latter to shape the policy, posture and institutional development for the future. Ham-fisted though this definition may appear, it makes certain presumptions about the role of the individual university very particularly in the domain of planning and budgeting, just as it also makes certain assumptions about the type of relationship which binds universities generally to society or to the community. And, furthermore, though the connection is more remote, certain assumptions are made about how the student estate is construed.

It is important to explore these dimensions a little further if only for the fact that they provide a powerful explanation for the rise of our community and, no less significant, they provide an explanation behind the initiatives which led up to our creation twenty five years ago.

ROOTS

It is very far from coincidental that the roots of institutional research lie not in Europe so much as in the United States and, to a lesser extent, the United Kingdom. In other words, institutional research is in part the product of a very particular relationship between universities and government on the one hand, and on the other the arrival of the higher education system to which it applies, at a specific stage in its development, namely massification. What set higher education in the United States from its European counterparts was not simply that it reached massification some three decades earlier.[1] It was also a series of systems in which functions that in Europe were located at central government level and under ministerial oversight, initiative and responsibility were embedded in the individual institution.[2] Amongst them, the setting of admissions standards, the determination of university fees, the conditions of hiring, revenue generation, the decision to launch new programmes or to terminate non-viable ones, internal budgetary allocation and above all that task which weighs upon the shoulders of American university Presidents – to wit, the raising of funds, the quest for donations and the hunt for endowments. (Fisher & Quehl 1989: 4) The development of an 'internal intelligence gathering capacity' – which is essentially what institutional research is about – becomes singularly important when student fees and thus the attraction of students form a substantial part not simply of the university budget [3] but also reflects the standing and repute of the establishment in the community. Institutional research becomes central both for shaping future institutional development and policy, for ascertaining and evaluating how far current policy is 'on track'. Institutional research was not confined, however, to what today would be termed 'internal audit'. But precisely because ties between university and local community in the United States were particularly strong and expressed in the various forms of Boards of Trustees – or in the public sector, Regents – institutional research played and, for that matter still plays – an essential part in shaping the terms and conditions under which the university negotiated and re-negotiated its place in that community (Trow 2003).

...AND ORIGINS IN EUROPE

The question this raises is, of course, when and how did institutional research begin to assume importance in Europe? Here, for very obvious reasons, both the circumstances and the general context were very different, and though it is safe to say that the drive to mass higher education certainly played its part, it did so through a very different angle d'approche. Put simply, whilst in the United States research into higher education at systems level evolved out of institutional research, in Britain and Europe the converse was the case: institutional research emerged in the wake of systems level investigation. More particularly, it finds its earliest origins in the various commissions of enquiry that were set up from 1958 onwards in Sweden and from 1961 onwards in Britain which governments had brought together to consider how best to deal with 'expanding social demand' for higher learning. (Neave 1989: 211–222.)

There are good reasons for these differences, not least of which the fundamental construct of the university as a service of state. This was a powerful interpretation and that on two counts. First, it had been fully assimilated into, and reinforced by the notion of, higher learning as part of the 'welfare state' – a policy that took shape in the period of post war reconstruction. (Neave 1992) Second, higher learning, construed in this light, built upon a far earlier notion that had accompanied the emergence of the modern university in Europe from the first two decades of the 19th century. This particular functional interpretation formed the bedrock of both the Napoleonic and the Humboldtian model of university. Both stood as a state service, supported by government monies and subject to a high degree of operational oversight by central national administration. Such oversight extended entre autres to appointments, conditions of employment and student admission, which were largely set out in a framework, of national application and grounded in administrative or constitutional law. The fact that universities in Europe were construed in this light largely accounts for the relative tardiness – relative, that is to the United States – in the emergence of institutional research.

ACCOUNTING FOR TARDINESS

This tardiness can be explained with reference to a number of factors, the first of which was that as a state service, universities in Europe could count on public finance for their development. And whilst they had most certainly to render accounts for the use of that money, such accountability was limited in scope, and is sometimes alluded to as a 'closed cycle' concept of accountability. It involved, essentially, a relationship of financial probity with the appropriate Ministry and the verification that expenditure had been undertaken in keeping with current legislative stipulation. This is not to say competition was absent between institutions. But if it took a public form, that public competition was equally limited and confined largely to the area of the 'glittering prizes' of research and research funding. Nor in Europe did competition involve universities locked in strife for students. Effectively, the drive towards massification in Europe stood as the polar opposite of the situation in the United States. For if in the latter instance, institutions competed for students and no less for the fees that came with them, in the former, it was students who competed for places. Indeed, in certain systems, competition for places was itself tied not to admission to university so much as to the results obtained in the Upper Secondary school leaving certificate. (Teichler

1985) Such was the case in both France and Germany, where, for the duly qualified places in higher education were guaranteed by the weight of constitutional law. And if fees were charged, which was not always the case, [4] often they amounted to little more than token payments and in certain systems, were not even paid fully by either the students or their families.[5] And, finally, it is worth recalling that public funding of higher education in Europe until the crisis of the so-called oil shock that rippled through higher education in the Seventies was based on inputs and on per capita funding.

Seen from this perspective, the drive to massification in Europe was a wholly government initiative to which higher education responded with varying degrees of lamentation and the wringing of hands. And with the infinite wisdom that looking backwards provides us, very little of the basic relationship between government, higher education and society changed in respect of procedures or instrumentality of control. Certainly the scale of the undertaking and the yearly leap-frogging of student numbers throughout the 1960s and on towards the mid 1970s, was unprecedented in the history of the university in Europe. Massification was, then, construed as extending the provision of a state service. It emerged as the Nation investing in the younger generation, tapping what was then presented as the 'reserves of talent'. The guiding ethic was very far from being that of competition. Nor was the burden on the individual universities seen in these terms either. For whilst economic efficiency minced up and down the catwalk of policy, such notions of efficiency as accompanied it were held to reside in terms of social justice, a social justice that sought to enhance individual opportunity by publicly removing the obstacles that lay across the path of access to higher learning.

THE RISE OF RESEARCH INTO HIGHER EDUCATION

The decision of governments to move towards mass higher education laid down the roots of higher education research, of policy research at systems level and, later the emergence of institutional research. In other words, it created the beginnings of the higher education research community – and very particularly in Britain and Sweden. To give the obvious illustrations, in Britain the creation of the Prime Minister's Committee of Enquiry into Higher Education, chaired by the economist, Lionel Robbins was one such mobilising event. The series of Government Commissions in Sweden from 1958 onwards looked into such matters as the implications of mass higher education for academic recruitment and staffing. 10 years later, following the rousing Events in the Paris of May 1968, another major Commission was rushed into place.

The U68 Commission was charged with a wide-scale review of the Swedish university. Its mandate focused on such matters as the structure of the undergraduate curriculum structure, the place of training for research, the spatial distribution of higher education, admissions policy and very particularly the objective to extend access to higher education to older age groups. (Premfors 1983) These were marker events not simply because in the case of Britain, they brought the systematic study of higher education into the groves of academe – the Higher Education Research Unit, which settled into the London School of Economics, under the leadership of Claus Moser, serviced the Robbins Committee. In Sweden, the emergence of research in higher education took a slightly different path. It was primarily the outcome of creating a separate Board for Higher Education – the Office of the Chancellor of the Swedish Universities (UHÄ) in 1967 and the subsequent establishment of a higher education research programme on the one hand and a Follow Up programme on the other. (Jenkinson & Neave 1983) The former concentrated on the long-term perspective at systems level. The latter as its name suggests, focused on immediate issues, particularly in the areas of student learning, through put and achievement.

THE EARLIEST ORIGINS CONTRASTED: BRITAIN AND SWEDEN

This situation gives us an insight into the early origins of institutional research in Britain and Sweden. There were, however, certain obvious differences between the part institutional research played in these two settings. In Sweden, the FoU programme served as a species of follow up monitor of the reforms outlined by the U68 Commission. It was conducted both inside the Office of the Chancellor of the Swedish Universities – the administrative Board with oversight for higher education, created in 1967 – with individual projects out-sourced to university departments. Institutional research monitored the immediate short- term effects of policy in terms of student flows, performance, through put and learning. Both organisationally and budgetarily, it stood apart from the programme on Research into Higher Education. The latter's main task lay in exploring higher education policy at system level and from a long-term forward-looking perspective. It concentrated on resourcing, governance, and relations between the higher education system, government and society.

Though one may detect what was essentially a similar line of demarcation in Britain between system-focused research and its institutional counterpart, the distinction between the two was more complex in origin. Certainly, the initiative to support higher education research at system level had, as we have seen, its origins at the highest level. But the origins of institutional research in the British context owed more to developments inside individual universities than it did to official support. Certainly, institutional research à l'anglaise contained a monitoring function. It did not, however, take the form of monitoring along lines set out by government so much as by the institutions themselves. In the early phase of its development; institutional research revolved around three main concerns: the advent and progress of 'the new student', the development of new teaching techniques and what generally passed under the rubric of 'staff development'. In effect, institutional research in Britain had as its prime focus the paedagogical adjustment of the individual university to an expansion the main impact of which was held to lie in bringing in the 'reserves of talent'. These reserves were operationally defined as students coming from those sections of society with no previous experience of higher education. The main burden of institutional research in Britain lay then less in following up the agreed lines of reform. Rather it was more internally focused - assisting institutions to adjust to what were felt to be the demands in teaching technique and thus staff training that the wave of 'new students' appeared to require.

At an intuitive level, that institutional research in Britain during the late Sixties and early Seventies should have invested in so narrow a range of activities may be explained by invoking particular aspects of what, from a European standpoint, may be seen as certain exceptional features in the relationship between government and universities. The first of these was the very particular system of financing. This involved a system by which universities negotiated their overall budget collectively with the Treasury (Ministry of Finance) through the University Grants Committee. The UGC subsequently distributed the yearly budget to individual universities on a lump sum basis. The responsibility for internal allocation rested fully in the hands of the individual establishment. This system, unique in Europe, has been described in terms of a 'philanthropic' relationship (Williams 1986) that is, governments virtually underwrote the bill presented by universities. The second aspect – and it was no less important – admission to British universities was wholly governed by a numerus clausus. Eligibility to enter was very far from denoting acceptance, for indeed acceptance lay in the hands of the individual departments to which a student applied. In other words, British universities controlled and regulated student demand in keeping with their individual and particular capacities. In turn, they were able to regulate their capacities in keeping with the resources that their main channel of negotiation with the government procured them. Simply stated, in Britain, the origins of institutional research, unlike the United States, did not, in the first instance, derive from the principle of competition. Nor was it, as in Sweden, the direct outcome of the wish of government to keep track of the progress of reform. Competition posed no problem at all, because, as we have pointed out, it operated on the student body, not the institution.

THE THIRD WAY

There is, even so, a third variant in Europe. It too is well worth taking into account, if only for the fact that we cannot always assume that institutional research or the intelligence gathering by institutions on their specific condition, is necessarily present or has followed the same developmental pathways as it did, for instance, in Britain and Sweden. In both Britain and Sweden, the setting up of government committees of enquiry 'primed the pump' for research into higher education both at the systems and at the institutional level. The former, as we have seen, did so by dint of setting up a specific programme and harnessing the skills available in the university. The latter opened up a window of opportunity, which encouraged individual universities and individuals within them to turn their attention to this new opportunity. By no means all governments viewed the drive for growth in the same way. Nor did they go very far along the road in encouraging research into higher education as a coherent undertaking. In such systems amongst which the best – or depending on one's personal view, the worst – examples were, curiously, precisely those where the student influx was the most unbridled – France, Italy and Spain. It is, however, only fair to point out that Spanish higher education remained in the glacial grip of dictatorship until 1976. (Garcia Garrido, 1992) This is not to say that research into higher education in those three systems was utterly and desolatingly absent. But it remained rather, the work of isolated individuals. In short, the functional equivalent of both systems analysis and institutional research did not emerge from the place where it had long resided – that is to say, within the particular Ministry responsible for higher education or, in the absence of such a body, the appropriate section within the National Ministry of Education.[6] In stark contrast to Britain and Sweden, there was little attempt to engage higher education in self-study or to extend that technical capacity far beyond the corridors of ministerial power. And from this it follows that the forces which eventually contributed to the emergence of institutional self-investigation were not only later in manifesting themselves. They were driven by considerations of a very different order. If the first glimmerings of institutional research were to be seen in Britain and Sweden in the late Sixties and early Seventies, it is probably correct in the case of France, Spain and Italy to see the grounding of institutional research as the product of the past decade and a half. In other words, within the particular world of institutional research, there was indeed a 'Europe a deux vitesses.' For these three countries, massification was not without its turbulence and uproar. Such an enviable state was attained nevertheless, within the administrative framework and close grip of central government that had long been characteristic of these three systems. Whilst massification stimulated the early steps along the pathway towards institutional research in the case of Britain and Sweden, in the case of France, Spain and Italy stimulus came from a different quarter.

DIFFERENT PERSPECTIVES AND INTERPRETATIONS

There are, to be sure, many ways to analyse the rise of institutional research in these three systems. On the one hand, it is often presented as part of that process identified with the 'professionalisation' of university administration, that is to say, the assumption of responsibilities that earlier had been under the purlieu of the central Ministry and the corresponding growth in specialist personnel and in the organisational complexity of the tasks discharged. Another factor contributing to the same process is the increasing importance attached to the regional community – a development, which in Spain was closely identified with the democratisation of higher education and the transfer of a large degree of both financial and administrative responsibility to the Autonomous Communities and away from Madrid, a strategy which, began in the mid 1980s and accelerated from the early 1990s onward. (Coombes & Perkins 1987; De Miguel, Gines-Mora & Rodriguez 1991) Similar moves are evident in France and very particularly with the passing of the 1989 Loi d'Orientation which introduced the principle of 'contractualisation' – that is, a system of financial tendering – on the one hand and strengthening the powers of Regional Councils in higher education policy on the other. (Neave 1999a: 31–65) In Italy too, the reform of higher education, carried out in 1997 and 1998, tends in a similar direction. It strengthened university-region ties by setting up University Regional Committees. This initiative is presented by some as a first step in a strategy designed to replace a modus operandi based on the historic top down, legalistically defined and determined system of higher education by one driven through bottom up initiatives, generated at institutional level, rapid, responsive and flexible (Varia 2003).

REGIONALISATION

Certainly, such reforms may be seen as breaking the historic ties of centralisation and reducing the principle of 'legal homogeneity' (Neave & Van Vught 1994) as the prime instruments by which systems change is brought about.   And, from within the administrative history of these three systems, such a move was clearly a watershed of a very major kind indeed.   But if we look at these developments from the standpoint of the consequences they hold for institutional research, we begin to appreciate their true significance.   Regionalisation not only increases the numbers of formal stakeholders. By assigning them elements of financial responsibility, it also imposes the obligation upon universities to extend their nexus of accountability to them.   In addition, it multiplies what might be termed 'proximate' stakeholders – regional authorities – in addition to the traditional and more distant ones – to wit the Ministry.   In the case of Spain, the powers of the Autonomous Communities, which even extend to having their own Evaluation Committees, has given rise to a rare situation in which the most proximate stakeholder is also the major one.

Regionalisation, strengthening of an intermediary layer between national administration and institution, has sometimes been looked upon as a revolution incomplete – a botched solution in which the Prince promised to enhance institutional autonomy and then had second thoughts. (Neave 1999b) There is, however, another dimension, which if often examined as a separate issue, when viewed in conjunction with the development of institutional research assumes a rather different role. This second issue is the Rise of the Evaluative State. (Henkel & Little 1994; Neave 1998) One of prior conditions of moving higher education on from the time-honoured historic relationship with governments in Europe – namely as a state service - and to redefine it in terms of a 'public service' is – if one cares to think about it in these terms – dependent upon creating a 'competitive mentality'. Or, to put matters slightly differently, such a radical transformation requires that the notion of 'competition' become the central ethical, strategic and operational bedrock in driving institutional development. However, as we remarked earlier in this essay, competition – save in the area of research tendering – was less an instrument to be utilised by Europe's universities so much as a situation to be mastered by them.   How then was the competitive mentality to be made the touchstone of an operationally efficient and an entrepreneurially responsive academia?

THE EVALUATIVE STATE: PRIMING THE COMPETITIVE MENTALITY

The clue lies in the rush towards setting up formal evaluation systems, an initiative lead in mainland Europe by the French in 1985, (Staropoli 1987) shortly followed by the Dutch who, in 1987 assigned this responsibility to the main national university committee – the Vereniging der Samenwerkende Nederlandse Universiteiten (VSNU) (Union of Co-operating Dutch Universities). By the mid 1990s, few if any systems of higher education in the European Union did not possess a specialist agency, para statal or organ with oversight for systematic evaluation. (Scheele, Maassen & Westerheijden 1997)

Evaluation, league tables and performance indicators can – and do - vary in their precision and lend themselves to interpretations that are all too rarely consensual. But they provide the basic information on which comparison can be made – however contentious the interpretation that may result.   More to the point, evaluation procedures have a dramatic impact upon institutional research itself. In those systems, like the British and the Swedish, where institutional research had already taken root, evaluation served to enlarge its scope and its field of application, moving it beyond the monitoring of student flows, background, subject choice, performance and graduation to embrace the performance and productivity of academic staff, to finance, cost surveillance, to institutional efficiency.   The advent of the Evaluative State, viewed from the particular standpoint of institutional research, conferred upon the latter a permanent and virtually compulsory status. It also transformed its operational location, siting it firmly at the heart of the systems of both public accountability and institutional decision-making.

   In those systems, like the French and Spanish, the rise of the Evaluative State had, if anything, an even greater impact. Not only did it make institutional self- assessment a key element in the 'professionalisation' of institutional administration and management.   It was also conceived as fundamental lever by which the individual institution could develop the instrumentality and intelligence-gathering capacity indispensable if it were to display those much vaunted virtues of adaptability, flexibility and rapidity of response to the demands of external stakeholders. In short, the introduction of institutional research into the groves of Academe, if it took place later, it did so as an integral part of the managerial revolution.

THE PUBLIC AND PRIVATE LIVES OF INSTITUTIONAL RESEARCH

Here it is, I would suggest, important to make the analytical distinction between institutional intelligence gathering that responds to the demands of national agencies of Evaluation and that which is generated by the particular demands within the institution itself. Certainly, institutional intelligence gathering lies at the heart of both. But it also feeds two very different purposes. The first places institutional research as part of that public function of demonstrating how individual universities have performed and have met public needs and priorities. The criteria involved, however, are not conceived within the institution. They are rather drawn up by the appropriate agency, which may bring various forms of suasion, sometimes not always moral, to ensure they are complied with. The public life of institutional intelligence gathering stands at the centre of the competitive ethic. It also has consequences for the institution. For whilst not all systems of evaluation are directly pegged to the allocation of financial resources, most assuredly they have direct and not always pleasant consequences for that most sensitive of all areas – the repute, standing, self-perception and excellence that the individual university has of itself. Thus, performance and institutional achievement today have public consequence which, in earlier days, they tended not to have to the same degree or, for that matter, with the same immediacy.

   It is in the logic of both the competitive ethic and the 'new relationship' between government and higher education, often summarised in terms of 'remote steering' (Van Vught 1988) that the individual university must have the means to develop its own strategy in the light of its own self assigned and negotiated objectives and the means, if need be, to modify it. Competition without adjustment, revision or modification is not far distant from sin without either repentance or contrition – a condition theologically dubious and operationally nonsensical. Indeed, the private life of institutional research – that is institutional research stricto sensu – brought to bear upon shaping priorities within the individual university is no less vital. Developing the 'private life' of institutional research functioning in its capacity as the handmaiden to policy, whether defined as institutional monitoring or as a dimension in the strategic management of the institution, is a more delicate task. Responding to the demands of the Prince - or his servants – is one thing. But precisely because institutional research in its 'private dimension' can, depending on where it is located and the tasks it is assigned, have direct effects on the balance of power between management and academia, it does not always follow that the capacity to gather intelligence for external consumption is necessarily reflected in its ability to do so for 'internal use'. Some systems, and the French is a good example, have embarked on a strategy that deliberately seeks to use institutional research acting in its public external function to stimulate its extension to the private domain – a strategy which acknowledges implicitly that, in the latter domain, much remains to be achieved (Neave 2002).

ENVOI

In this chapter, I have set out to place the development of institutional research against a rather broader canvas, that of the effect upon the development of our domain of policy change at the macro level. I have sought to do this in terms of the long term dynamic that underpinned the place of institutional research by referring, briefly to the situation in the United States and to its early origins in Western Europe. I have done so by drawing on Britain and Sweden and finally, by examining the implications that follow from changes in the traditional relationship between national administration and the university world in France, Spain and Italy.

From this we see that institutional research has taken different pathways which, if they lead the EAIR "on to fortune", display considerable contextual variation depending on the particular national system in which they have evolved and become rooted. Paradoxically, institutional research is not always the product of institutional initiative. In certain countries – Spain and France are noteworthy here – the stimulus has come from government. And even in those countries like Britain where initiatives first came from within higher education itself, the drive towards intelligence gathering has been urged forward by that broader strategy in which government seeks to inject competition by acting itself as a species of pseudo-market.

In all this, one thing stands out. Not only is the world higher education now serves more complex - student constituencies expand, stakeholders multiply, institutions diversify and financial resources come to resemble the crock at rainbow's end – always one field beyond one's grasp! It is also to an increasing extent a world which is highly unstable, though very often such instability is presented in clichés as empty as they are optimistic, as part of the university's current lot. The speed of change is one; the permanency of change is another. To be sure, this should not lead us to the ancient Heraclitan lament that 'All is in flux'. But it does require us to pay a little more attention to that other classical adage from the same stable, namely, 'Know Thyself'. This applies as much to the individual academic as it does to the establishment of which she – or he – is the prime human resource. Institutional research is an excellent way of ensuring both over the coming quarter of a century if not beyond!

NOTES

[1] The usual tipping point from elite to mass higher education is commonly held to have occurred with the surge in enrollment in higher education by returning servicemen at the end of World War II, a development that followed directly on from the passing of the 'Servicemen's Re-adjustment Act", the so called 'GI Bill of Rights', in 1944. There is, however, some indication that the magical 15 % of the relevant age group entering higher education was exceeded in 1940. *(personal communication from Martin Trow, March 2001)* For the rationale of the 15 % as the threshold between elite and mass higher education see Martin Trow [1974] 'Problems in the Transition from Elite to Mass Higher Education' in OECD *From Elite to Mass Higher Education,* Paris, OECD 2 vols.

[2] In some State University systems, the system wide administration is so complex that it rivals in size the Ministry of Education of certain small European Nations. Thus in the 1980s the system wide administration of the University of California occupied one of the few six story buildings in the City of Berkeley.

[3] How important this particular item is in American university budgets can be gathered when one considers for instance that in 1985 for private universities student fees accounted for some 54.8 % of revenue and for 17.5 % in public institutions. (Stadtman, 1992: 783, Table 3.) Even today, the latter statistic is rarely achieved in Western Europe, save in one or two *établissements d'exception.*

[4] This is still the case in Germany even today, though the threat of serious reconsideration now hangs over the student estate in that country.

[5] For example, in the United Kingdom, where today the eagerness for 'full cost fees' is exceeded only by Australia, university fees during the 1960s, though subject to a parental incomes test, were paid by the individual's Local Education Authority, that is, by the municipality where the student's family had its residence and to which it paid local taxes.

[6] For a closer examination of this see Guy Neave (2001) *Educacion Superior: historia y politica - Estudios comparativos sobre la universidad contemporanea,* Barcelona, Gedisa, pp. 25 – 27.

REFERENCES

Coombes, P. & Perkins, J. A. (1987). *La Reforma universitaria espanola: evaluacion et informe,* Madrid, Consejo de Universidades.

De Miguel, Gines-Mora, S. (1991*). La Evaluacion de las institutiones universitarias,* Madrid, Consejo de Universidades.

Fisher, J. L. & Quehl, Gary H. (1989). *The President and Fund-raising,* New York, Macmillan.

Garcia Garrido, J-L. Spain. In: Clark, Burton R. & Neave, Guy R. (1992). *The Encyclopedia of Higher Education.* Oxford: Pergamon.

Henkel, M. & Little, B. (1984). *The Evaluative State.* London, Jessica Kingsley.

Jenkinson, S. & Neave, G. R. *Higher Education research in Sweden: an analysis and an evaluation.* Stockholm: Almqvist & Wiksell International.

Metzger, W. P. (1987). The Academic Profession in the United States. In: Clark, Burton R. (ed.), *The Academic Profession: National, Disciplinary and Institutional Settings* (pp. 123 – 210). Berkeley/Los Angeles/London: University of California Press.

Neave, G. R. (1989). Foundation or roof? The qualitative, structural and institutional dimensions in the study of Higher Education. *European Journal of Education,* 24(3), 211- 222.

Neave, G. R. (1992). War and educational reconstruction in Belgium, France and the Netherlands, 1940-1947. In: Roy Lowe (ed.), *Education and the Second World War* (pp. 84-127). London: Falmer Press.

Neave, G. R. (1998). The Evaluative State Reconsidered, *European Journal of Education,* 33(3), 265 - 284.

Neave, G. R. (1999a). Utilitarianism by increment: Disciplinary differences and higher education reform in France. In: Claudius Gellert (ed.), *Innovation and adaption in higher education: the changing conditions of advanced teaching and learning in Europe* (pp. 31 – 65). London: Jessica Kingsley.

Neave, G. (1999b). Some thoughts on the fin de siècle university, Address to the 5th ALFA-BRACARA *Conference Higher Education: the last 5 years and the challenges for the future,* (pp. 23), Universidade Federal do Ceará, Fortaleza, Brazil, July 21-23.

Neave, G. (2000). *Educacion Superior: historia y politica - Estudios comparativos sobre la universidad contemporanea* (pp. 25 – 27). Barcelona: Gedisa.

Neave, G. R. (2000). *The Temple and its Guardians: An Excursion into the Rhetoric of Evaluating Higher Education.* Address to the Institute for Democratic Education. Tokyo.

Neave, G. R & Van Vught, F. A. (1994). *Prometeo Encadenado: estado y educación superior en Europa.* Barcelona: Gedisa.

Premfors, R. R.T (1984). *Higher Education Organization: conditions for policy implementation.* Stockholm: Almqvist & Wiksell International.

Scheele, J. P. Maassen, P. A.M. & Westerheijden, D. F. (eds.) (1998). *To Be Continued...follow up of Quality Assurance in Higher Education.* The Hague: Elsevier/De Tijdstroom.

Stadtman, V. (1992). The United States. In: Clark, Burton R. & Neave, Guy R., *The Encyclopedia of Higher Education.* Oxford: Pergamon.

Staropoli, A. (1987). The French National Committee of Evaluation, *European Journal of Education*, 22(3).

Teichler, U. (1985). Germany. In: Clark, Burton R. (ed.), *The School and the university: an international perspective.* Berkeley/Los Angeles/London:University of California Press.

Trow, M (1974). Problems in the transition from Elite to Mass Higher Education. In: OECD, *From Elite to Mass Higher Education,* Paris: OECD.

Trow, M. (2003). In Praise of Weakness: Chartering, the University of the United States and Dartmouth College. *Higher Education Policy,* 16(1).

Van Vught, F. A. (1988). *Self-evaluation, self-study and program review in Higher Education.* Culemborg: Lemma.

Varia, M. (2003). Higher education reform in Italy 1996 - 2001: an institutional analysis and a first appraisal 1996 – 2001. *Higher Education Policy,* 16(2).

Williams, G. (1996). *Paying for Education beyond Eighteen: an evaluation of issues and options.* London: Council for Industry and Higher Education.

RODDY BEGG AND CHARLES BELANGER

EAIR IN THE MAKING

Abstract. This chapter attempts to bring to life the early years of the movement that became EAIR, by recounting Forum events, colourful anecdotes, growing pains and important decisions. Conceived in an era when globalisation, personal computers and the internet did not exist, EAIR evolved from its early AIR parentage years to a fully-fledged independent organisation serving the professional needs of its individual members, in particular through its annual Forum and its journal – Tertiary Education And Management (TEAM).

To attain the Truth, we need, once in our life, to get rid of all the opinions we received and to build again, from the foundations, all the systems of our knowledge.
René Descartes

NOVEMBER 1979

On the 16th of November 1979, the symbol was striking. Twenty-six (26) individuals from 12 different countries and two continents, gathered in the Descartes Amphitheatre located inside the walls of the Old Sorbonne, were being welcomed, in prophetic terms, by the President of one of the largest universities in France:

> Tradition is of little use (unless) we discover and apply qualitative and quantitative techniques which enable us to answer this double challenge: to become better and better with less and less resources and to prove it.

> It is sure that European administrators, managers and researchers in the field of higher education systems improvement have a lot to learn in contact with AIR representatives. But it does not mean that it would be a one-way co-operation. ...perhaps we, Europeans also have many things to show and teach North Americans. (Ahrweile 1979: 5-6).

A merger of contrasts was in the making: the 'high' culture of the old countries with the 'experimental' culture of the young continent; the more ideological tenet of the university concept as a society-shaping institution with the more utilitarian approach to higher education as a professional and socio-economic lever; and the accustomed way of managing public institutions tied to government methods and riches with the less travelled style dictated by greater autonomy and diversified financial sources. Even before the welcome address of the First Forum, participants from both sides of the ocean knew that their differences were strands apart, and yet that they shared many of the same concerns and interests. The unknown was really how many of 'them-us' would be willing to listen first, consider second, and then decide that by engaging in a dialogue, 'their-our' professional and institutional predicaments, as so vividly captured by President Ahrweiler, would be enhanced.

Compelled as we are to reflect on our historical antecedents as a special interest community, let us remind ourselves that facts alone can bore us to death - while embellished anecdotes can easily take legendary proportions. Hopefully this chapter will be a tribute to those 'pioneers' who had to go down memory lane to recollect

R. Begg (ed.), The Dialogue between Higher Education Research and Practice, 15–30.
© 2003 *Kluwer Academic Publishers. Printed in the Netherlands.*

important events and unrepeatable episodes, particularly in the early years of this organisation to help these two authors to bring life and veracity to 25 years of existence. It is also an occasion for newer EAIR members to realise that non-profit professional organisations are not unlike small businesses. The ones that do survive and thrive are the results of foresight, hard work, luck, need fulfilment, and shrewd change management from committed leadership and membership. EAIR is a living proof of that.

THE INCUBATING YEARS (1975-1979)

Independent testimonies confirm that what became EAIR was conceived in California during the AIR San Diego Forum, in May 1979, either at the Balboa Zoo during a spectacle of trained birds or at a French wine and goat cheese party by the poolside. Thereafter, the involved protagonists played a steady parental role in the early years with various contributions. First, a few words about how the courting season evolved. American 'institutional researchers' incorporated their Association for Institutional Research (AIR) in May 1965. From 384 charter members in its first year, AIR grew rapidly not only in numbers but also in vitality and sophistication (Doi 1979). A decade later, it was clear that Institutional Research (IR) had convincingly emerged as a staff function and a profession in North American universities (Tetlow 1973; 1979; Johnson 1979). In return for their membership fees, members insisted on more services and support. It was in 1975 that an AIR Professional Development and Services Committee (PDS) was set up, with a Workshops Subcommittee and an International Activities Subcommittee (IAS), both chaired by F. Craig Johnson, Professor of IR at Florida State University. The workshop side of the Committee was quickly a smashing success with a first workshop in Atlanta followed by many other sites.

Expectations for the international activities were less clear and represented a priority that did not quite register on the radar screen of the typical AIR member and elected Board official whose daily livelihood depended almost entirely on the resolution of institutional and local problems, with the occasional exposure to regional and perhaps national (USA) issues. After all, perestroïka and glasnost were still a decade away from appearing on the scene, and globalisation had not surfaced as a household name. What then was the rationale behind establishing a subcommittee to oversee international activities that only a small faction of members were passionate about? Was it savvy, greed, or just dumb luck? Probably a combination of all three! In the mid-1970s, AIR already counted close to 1200 members with about half of them attending the annual Forum. Although the Canadian membership was on the rise (around 100 members), numbers from other parts of the world were stagnating at around 25 to 30 and showing no sign of improvement. Only the odd 'foreigner' from Asia, Australia, Europe or Latin America attended occasional annual AIR Forums. However, as overall AIR membership increased, so did the appetite for more growth, more services and more revenue. The European market was perceived as a potential target for new recruits. The problem was that, having approved its own resolution without fully understanding the consequences, AIR remained a reluctant player, had no experience in the international arena, had a collective knowledge of the European terrain over which no one could have tripped, was widely assuming that Europeans were doing no institutional research, and therefore saw itself as the only game in town: 'Y' all come and learn!' The plan resulted in four years of sputtering while only the few international 'zealots' (including a handful of Americans) kept hammering away at the issue. Understandably, the overwhelming majority did not really mind or notice as they were too busy adding student-credit hours, producing induced course load matrices, and crunching numbers because students had to be counted and retained, budgets prepared, policies documented, etc … and these were their immediate concerns. The elected AIR Board leaders, as in most professional organisations, were themselves clones of the membership. Knowing how other countries were struggling with (perhaps) the same issues and comparing notes had little place, if any, in their universe.

At least, those four years (1975-1979) had served to confirm one thing. AIR had sent a Board member twice to Europe to join an international group interested in Higher Education as a field of study. The event was run like an organised tour. Fifty people paid a conference fee, for which they had room and board, a chance to present and publish a paper and, at the end, a tax receipt. That exclusive group met every summer in a different location, presented papers that lacked peer review and whose substance was of mixed rigour and limited interest. If European activities ever took off, the Love Boat tour model was not it! During the same period, there had also been two reciprocal visits from OECD-IMHE and AIR representatives to participate into each other's events. After four years of distant and lackadaisical courtship, the historical conception moment was on the cusp.

FROM HATCHING TO INFANCY (1979-1981)

The attractive venue of the San Diego Forum had contributed to drawing together a number of elements favourable to making 16 November, 1979 a memorable date. The incoming AIR President, F. Craig Johnson who was a strong supporter of the international movement, had indicated several months in advance who, among Board members, was going to chair available committees and subcommittees, as previous practice wanted it, and encouraged every one to start developing terms of reference, goals and strategies so as to be able to have a productive first meeting under his one-year tenure. That procedure provided every Board member with an adequate time allocation to explain his/her plans, and for the first time, elevated the International Activities Subcommittee to a more level playing field. The IAS was now chaired by Charles Bélanger (from 1979 to 1982), then Director of IR at the University of Montreal, and someone who had studied under Johnson and shared similar ambitions. Concurrently, Claude Cossu, Professor of Management Science at the Université de Paris 1 (Sorbonne) was discussing his interest in organising the 'First AIR European Forum in Paris' with other European colleagues present in greater numbers at the San Diego Forum: Aidan Duggan from the Royal Irish Academy, Thaly Nilsson from Uppsala Universitet, Michel Hecquet from Université Catholique de Louvain, John Calvert from Loughborough University of Technology, and Paul Levasseur from OECD–IMHE. AIR Board members, who did not feel ready in May to authorise the Paris Forum, took a deep breath, crossed their fingers, and approved the project at their September meeting, giving two months to organise and improvise the Paris meeting. Fortunately, before leaving San Diego, it had been decided that those involved in the discussions would serve as regional 'correspondents' as well as IAS members. For rapid communications, telegraph and telephone (rotary of course!) were still the instruments of choice and both were used abundantly.

Out of the 26 participants at the First Forum, there were 21 Europeans (only four AIR members), three Americans, and two Canadians. Half of them were Heads/Directors/VPs of Administration, and the other half divided between professors and directors of institutional research. Interestingly enough, the overwhelming majority of the 21 European participants had been involved in a multi-country university costing study led by IMHE between 1972 and 1975. The First Proceedings (Cossu, 1979) constitute an accurate record of the Programme, the list of participants, and the formal presentations. Obviously, what falls outside the scope of any conference proceedings is the spirit and substance of discussions, the camaraderie, as well as occasional odd occurrences. There were some pretty straightforward statements made by the more senior European participants. Aidan Duggan was one of them:

> What benefits can be derived from convening a meeting such as this, of Europeans with an interest in Institutional Research in Europe, under the aegis of a body such as AIR?
>
> a)   Many of us meet in another Paris Forum, under the auspices of OECD–IMHE, but that body, while its meetings and seminars are open to all, is essentially institutional in membership, while we are here as <u>individuals</u>, addressing topics which interest us as professionals, as well as those which face our individual institutions today.
>
> b)   Because we are joined by five senior North American colleagues, we are given the chance to compare our European systems with those of the U.S. and Canada and hopefully gain new insights into both. I have spoken before of the obverse of today's meeting, when European members of AIR attend the Forum in North America. Far too often our participation was restricted to a ghetto-like 'Special Interest' meeting of ourselves, or to intervene at the end of a detailed discussion and say "But we do that differently in Europe" and, if given time, explain exactly how. My main theme...is not (to talk about) the <u>differences</u> between North America and Europe, but the <u>similarities</u>... (Duggan 1979: 21-22).

Aidan had attended several AIR Forums and knew, like half of the audience, that IR was the application of various research methods and techniques to collect and analyse data in order to quantify an institution's performance and determine to what degree it was fulfilling its stated goals. The difficulty was with the other 50% - who did not. They struggled to understand why this was called 'research' and why it was labeled 'institutional'. They claimed (and rightfully so, at least in the generalisation of the results) that this did not fit the known model of 'academic/disciplinary research'. One Danish Head of Administration confided to the audience that before being invited to this meeting he would have responded 'Don't know' if asked by a pollster if he knew what IR was. His statement tells the story:

> It may be difficult for our American friends to understand that up to now very little research has been done in the field of management of higher education...and I guess that this statement goes for other Scandinavian countries too. There are at least two reasons for that: Firstly, our countries are rather small with a limited research capacity in the field of management...Secondly...the administration of higher education has never been considered as something special. The administrative jobs have been considered as jobs of the same kind as the jobs of other civil servants and many Danish – and I guess Scandinavian – universities have very limited administrative resources compared with American universities, even if I admit that it is difficult to compare. (Carpentier 1979: 23).

What was interesting about the first day of that First Forum was that no matter what the topics of the presentations were, discussions had a tendency to revolve around one question: What is Institutional Research? Another anecdotal event contributed to relaxing the audience at the expense of the sanity of the two presenters involved. The two slide projectors that the Sorbonne provided seemed to almost literally implode, with traces of black smoke and smells of burnt plastic as in a display of fireworks, urging the presenters to consider Plan B in a hurry. The technician du jour learned that a reaction was bound to occur if 120 and 220 volts outlets were confounded.

The second and last day of the First Forum was dominated by three complementary items that cemented a few loose tiles. First, the presentation of three detailed Planning and Budgeting case studies (West Virginia University, Uppsala Universitet, and Université Catholique de Louvain) that showed the audience that not only was it possible to be different and yet to apply similar methods and techniques, but brought home the fact that many were involved in these kinds of activities, at least marginally. Edwin Smith (1979), associate vice-president administration from West Virginia, encapsulated best the diversity of approaches:

> ...it may be safely said that there are at least 60 different higher education budgeting systems in North America. That is, one for each of the 50 U.S. states and the 10 Canadian provinces. All of these will also give claim to having some formal planning systems...and no self-respecting institution would not admit to not planning. (p 54).

At that time, the only two institutions known to have American style offices of IR in Europe were Université Catholique de Louvain and Uppsala Universitet.

The second agenda item was about the internationalisation of AIR and possible structures that Europeans could envision. As pointed out by Bélanger (1979), Chair of the International Activities Subcommittee, AIR had no intention of changing its name, no interest in becoming a federation of associations, and European AIR members did not have the numbers sufficient to impact AIR decision-making or to form their own association. As a matter of practicality, if Europeans thought that there was something beneficial in this type of transatlantic exchange. They would have to reach a critical mass of AIR members in order to try to influence AIR directions and if that did not work, other options would come in due time. His concluding statement turned out to be prescient:

> There is no doubt in my mind that the results of the Paris meeting will have a determinant effect on whether we decide to go the insularity or the communication road. (Bélanger 1979: 89).

Thirdly, at the end of the Paris meeting, John Calvert made a spontaneous offer to host the Second European AIR Forum in London in 1980. That gesture proved to be a critical link to the future and represented the only decision reached at the Paris meeting. True, we had learned much about each other's problems and plans for solving them!

The 1980 (London) and 1981 (Louvain-la Neuve) Forums re-affirmed the interest of many of the same participants and saw new recruits join in the action. These early meetings were characterised by planning process, case studies and quantitative presentations by analysts and professors who talked freely with university administrators about methods for solving problems that had political implications. There was little inhibition as issues seemed to be confronted on neutral ground and to serve a much needed purpose. Leonard Kail, then Secretary of the University of Surrey put the early efforts into perspectives (2003):

> I started to attend AIR and EAIR forums soon after my appointment (as Secretary) at
> Surrey in 1980...Having come from a strong professional background outside the
> Universities I was rather dismayed at the lack of opportunities for younger staff to develop
> professional interests and to realise that they were part of a world wide activity which
> extended far beyond their own institutions.

The family atmosphere of the first three years had been a lesson in learning how to
walk.

SEARCHING FOR IDENTITY (1982-1988)

As much as the first three years had rested on very few shoulders, personal financial
contributions, and virtually no institutional support, the Uppsala Forum (1982)
demarcated itself from the previous ones with its more professional approach. A Call
for Papers was properly issued, an attractive Programme was printed and sent to
registrants, a pre-Forum professional development workshop was offered, a Forum
Evaluation Form was distributed, and the Local Arrangements Committee benefited,
for the first time, from much needed institutional support with secretarial and other
essential logistics. As more 'heavy weights' made their way into the Programme, more
participants also showed up, requiring for the first time the use of concurrent sessions.
Social events such as a town hall reception, an evening concert, and 'A Night by the
Sea' Forum Banquet with the typical Swedish 'smörgåsbord' reflected the elevated
sophistication of the event. The Forum Chair, Thaly Nilsson and his team had raised
the bar to a degree that subsequent Forum Chairs would find impossible to ignore.

Even the discussion had its animated moments. Those present at that Forum may
remember the very last session which was meant to mesh the main theme 'Universities
in a Changing World: Adaptation or Guidance?' with other presentations. The question
being debated by a Chancellor, a University President, and a President of a national
research council was how politically active a university should be. As all three agreed
that universities should not play a political role, Franz Bingen, from Vrije Universiteit
Brussel, stood up and presented them with a challenge: 'Our Universities opposed
Hitler during the 30s. In the 40s, Hitler invaded Brussels. His storm troops persecuted
our professors for years. Our opposition did not stop. We suffered. Where were you?'
Franz sat down to a long silence and the panel moved on to the next policy issue...

If the following Forum (1983), hosted by the Rijksuniversiteit Limburg in
Maastricht was equally successful, it was not for the structure allowing for continuity
from one year to the next. The annual meeting had become a serious professional event
with five theme tracks managed in picnic fashion. Each year a temporary organisation
had to be set up by a willing host university without the benefit of a permanent
structure that would pass on down the know how, the corporate memory, or minutes
of past meetings. The custom was for the Forum Chair of the previous year to transfer
a mailing list to his/her successor with his best wishes for success. Since membership
dues were still flowing to the (American) AIR head office, there was no financial
support per se except from registration fees and institutional commitment. Basic
document preparation was the ultimate responsibility of the Forum Chair and the host
institution.

As the European participants were gaining more assurance in the early 1980s, it
became obvious that AIR had no serious plan to make accommodations to its
governing and decision-making structure for the new European reality as well as for

that of other continental groups (e.g. Australia, Latin America and Asia). The status quo was then interpreted as indifference by veteran European and early North American leaders who grew increasingly uncomfortable with the relationship. Winds of secession were rising. Hans Acherman, then Senior Policy Advisor for the Dutch University System, was one of the quiet but influential voices behind systematically pursuing the big question: Why are we sending our money to AIR when we could use it to structure and organise ourselves in Europe? Due to the fact that there was no unanimous position among Europeans themselves on this issue, this question was going to consume much time during the following years and bring its dissenting moments. For the record, a meeting among Peter de Rooij (1983 Forum Chair), Frans van Vught (Director of the Center for Higher Education Policy Studies at the University of Twente) and Hans Acherman took place on 4 March, 1984 to examine the possibility of establishing a temporary and part-time secretariat/mail box at CHEPS. Shortly thereafter, in 1985, Peter Maassen, a new CHEPS researcher began his involvement with the Forum in that capacity.

Although the organisational structure had become a much discussed issue, the following Forums held at Vrije Universiteit Brussel (1984), Københavns Universitet (1985), Loughborough University of Technology (1986), University of Twente (1987) and University of Bergen (1988), kept enthusiasm on the rise and on the contagious list. Individuals were looking up to the Forum for their professional development. Participants frequently commented on the fortuitous mélange of qualitative and quantitative presentations that brought to the same table institutional researchers, policy analysts, scholars, university and agency executives, industrial executives, and government officials alike. At the Copenhagen Forum for instance, it was refreshing to hear from two distinguished Danish industrialists that, in addition to making money, the main purpose of their respective companies was to contribute to the social and cultural development of society. That Forum model was differentiating itself from the AIR meetings which were attended by a more homogeneous and technical crowd. The reason why that differentiation occurred had a great deal to do with the way institutional research functions were generally carried out in North America as opposed to Europe. In the former, functions were more specialised and compartmentalised while more integrated in the latter. For instance, AIR Forum themes in the mid-1980s revolved around the use of technology in IR offices as personal computers and decentralised databases were being introduced. Those at the European Forum had a much broader scope.

With time passing, it seems that the excellent programmes of those five Forums are now merged into one except for the social activities. Each host institution was trying to outdo the previous one … and they succeeded. Specific images stand in one's memory. The basement of the university building in Copenhagen that had been a student jail 500 years earlier. John Calvert dressed as Robin Hood and being chased by the Sheriff of Nottingham, his wife Mary. Students and alumni of the University of Bergen turning the pristine coastline of Norway into a live theatre. The sunken church of Twente inundated by a beer drinking student crowd. Or the Guinness World Record for the shortest financial report ever presented at a professional meeting (1984 Brussels Forum): Franz Bingen, a professor of Mathematics generally known as a man of a few words, stood up and wrote four letters on the board. 'A is what I was given from the last Forum, B is what I collected this year, C is what I will give to the next Forum, and E is for Epsilon or the population error term.' And Franz sat down to applause that lasted longer than his report. It is doubtful whether anyone will ever break his record ... or simply be allowed to try.

TAKING ITS OWN FLIGHT

The establishment of a temporary secretariat at Twente in 1985, proved to be another crucial milestone in EAIR's evolution. In the years preceding 1987-88, it was clear that Europeans had taken control of the organisation and that the AIR International Activities Subcommittee had over-extended its usefulness. Peter Maassen, who was serving as the 'part-time permanent' resident at the temporary secretariat, was in the process of consulting widely on both sides of the Atlantic on the Forum's future directions. Should it cut loose from AIR or negotiate some kind of win-win arrangement that would be reflected in the levy of fees and provision of services? Should it have a mostly technical focus on American style institutional research, or a more inclusive one in the field of higher education? Where should a Secretariat be located? In hindsight, practices of the last few years had already answered all those questions. However, agreeing on what seemed to be a fait accompli was a Herculean task. Leonard Kail made this observation (2003):

> I rapidly learned that cooperation in setting up a European organisation required a good deal of patience and much explanation as we tried to draft a Constitution. The English language, although widely used, seemed to be somewhat differently interpreted according to the nationality of the speaker!

Nevertheless, after circulating a proposal that suggested CHEPS as the first base for a permanent Secretariat, Leonard was asked to assume the chairmanship of a now incorporated and independent EAIR, a position he held to the date of his retirement in 1992.

It was now evident that over the years, the Forum had created its own momentum. Subsequent Forums, such as Trier (1989) and Lyon (1990) broke attendance records with approximately 400 participants. At that particular juncture, times were ripe for European initiatives of all kinds and participation from Eastern Europe was increasing. Coincidently, it was also in 1990 that the World Wide Web linked universities across the world and facilitated instant and cheap communications.

From the very first Forums, the leaders had been discussing the possibility of creating some mechanism to allow presenters to share their papers and ideas with a wider audience and to use that as a professional development tool and a way of enlarging the body of knowledge of their profession. One major obstacle encountered was the fact that most professionals involved with IR and planning activities, as well as administrators had little or no experience in writing papers that would approach publishable quality, let alone how to present them to a larger audience. AIR had gone through those growing pains a decade earlier and its European offspring, in spite of its own vitality and sophistication, was not going to escape them. Only time, experience and guidance would be the problem solvers. So far Forum Proceedings had been the privileged communication vehicle and had served as an acceptable compromise and grooming tool.

THE NEW ASSOCIATION

So, by the late 1980s, the European participants in the Forum felt ready to fly solo. This was not a reverse American War of Independence ... but a fully fledged bird ready to fly the nest. At the Forum in 1988 it was decided to create a separate association and in late 1989 - after the Dutch lawyers involved had done their job with the drafting of a Constitution – the European Association for Institutional Research ... EAIR for short ... came into being. Initially, it described itself as 'a European Higher Education Society'; however, ten years later, it was agreed that this was overly modest, and 'a' was changed to 'the' – on the recommendation of the then outgoing Chairman, Kari Hyppönen.

What did the change involve? To the average Forum participant ... very little. However, the new association had acquired a powerful tool – continuity. This was because part of the transformation was the establishment of a modest Secretariat ... in the form of a part-time secretary, based initially at CHEPS. The Secretariat replaced (in part) the ad hoc arrangements set up each year at the Forum's host University. Frans van Vught volunteered his Centre as the infant association's cradle. Peter Maassen agreed to be EAIR's first Executive Secretary and to oversee the work of the Secretariat. Jacinte van Schaik became EAIR's first employee. The traditional handing over of the 'European Forum box' from one Forum Chair to the next was replaced by the handing over of the EAIR flag at the Forum banquet.

The Secretariat remained at CHEPS for the next seven years. In 1997 – for a variety of reasons (including that Enschede was not the easiest place in Europe to travel to to attend meetings) – the Secretariat moved hosts, to the University of Amsterdam, where EAIR still leases a spacious, well-appointed and sunlit room on the Oude Turftmarkt, overlooking the canal. In place of a part-time secretary, the employees grew in status and number, when Ella Kruzinga became the professional Manager of the Secretariat, with a part-time secretary of her own, and the role of the Secretary of EAIR could become less 'hands on' ... and could drop the prefix 'Executive'.

The management of the Association passed to an Executive Committee, consisting of nine elected members – each serving three years – meeting with the current and incoming Forum Chairs. The customary arrangements were made to achieve a regular rotation in the membership, and, since 1990, elections have been held each spring and three members have taken up/demitted office at the Forum (though many have served two - and even three - three-year terms).

The Constitution provided that the Committee should appoint its own officers – Chairman, Vice-Chairman, Executive Secretary, Treasurer and Forum Chair. In addition, a new ... described as 'honorary' ... office of President was created, with a two-year term of office.

At the 1990 Forum, the new Committee was constituted, consisting of: Leonard Kail, UK (Chairman); Edgar Frackmann, Germany (Vice-Chairman); Peter Maassen, The Netherlands (Executive Secretary); Laurence Denonfoux, France (Treasurer); Hans Acherman (The Netherlands), Marianne Bauer (Sweden), Livin Bollaert (Belgium), Poul Bonde (Denmark) and Edmund Utne (Norway) (Committee members). The first President, Sir William Taylor, Vice-Chancellor of Hull University in the UK, was installed.

The Constitution also provided for the award of Distinguished Membership of the Association. This power has been used sparingly – four times in nearly 15 years – and those so honoured have been Leonard Kail and Kari Hyppönen (Chairmen of the Executive Committee at critical periods), Ulrich Teichler (the only two-term holder of the office of President) and Burton Clark (the distinguished American scholar and frequent presenter at EAIR Forums – see below)

A full list of Officers of the Association, and details of the Forums, are contained in the Appendices. As emerges clearly, the role of the Forum Chair has always been central to EAIR's success and survival, and many of these dedicated supporters of EAIR went on to stand successfully for election as members of the Executive Committee and to become its officers.

In addition to the Executive Committee, the Forums were planned by Programme and Local Arrangements Committees, and Track Chairs; these were appointed each year to oversee the details of the Forum arrangements - choosing the keynote speakers, selecting the presentations in the Tracks, etc. As mentioned earlier, however, the main benefit of the setting up of the association and a Secretariat was the continuity on which other developments could be built. The Constitution set out the objectives of the Association – primarily encouraging research and collaboration in higher education and holding an annual Forum.

EXPANDING THE SERVICES

Once it had secured the Forums, the Executive Committee could concentrate on research and collaboration, and consider the enhancement of the benefits of membership. Gradually, four additional services emerged.

Firstly, a directory of membership was created and published (initially) annually, providing full contact details on all EAIR's current members. This was aimed at assisting in the vital business of 'networking' with colleagues in other countries, who shared research and professional interests and roles. This was emphasised in all systematic and informal feedback from members as the main benefit of attendance at Forums and membership of EAIR. This service later went on-line, and the much treasured EAIR Directories ceased to exist in paper form.

Secondly, a Newsletter was circulated twice a year – initially in 'duplicated' format and now more glossily printed. The Newsletters kept the members up to date with progress on Forum planning and the other activities stimulated by the Executive Committee.

Thirdly, ad hoc seminars on the 'hot topics' of the day have been arranged – in collaboration with a University. So far, four such seminars have been arranged, in Amsterdam (twice), Birmingham and Barcelona. The Barcelona Seminar on Governance in June 2000 was more like a conference, as it attracted 230 participants (representing 111 institutions, from 27 countries) to the Technical University of Catalonia. Its proceedings were published as the June 2001 issue of TEAM (see below). The seminar on employability of graduates, held in Amsterdam in June 2003, was the first to be held in collaboration with our parent association – AIR – as well as a host institution, the University of Amsterdam, which had housed EAIR's Secretariat, by then, for five years.

LAUNCHING THE JOURNAL

The fourth service EAIR provides to its members is its journal, Tertiary Education And Management (TEAM). From the early days, the Forum organisers attempted to publish the best of their papers as conference proceedings. However, these proceedings appeared irregularly, often long after the event, and enjoyed a limited circulation. Accordingly – in part stimulated by Napier publishing all the 1991 Forum papers in a volume weighing several kilos, that few could manage to carry home from Lyon! - in Turku in 1993, the Executive Committee agreed in principle to publish a journal; as happens so frequently in academic circles, the EC member who chaired the small working party that recommended the change, Roddy Begg of the University Aberdeen in Scotland, was asked to be the founding Editor. A London-based publisher, Jessica Kingsley, agreed to publish the journal on behalf of the association, and TEAM Volume 1 Number 1 appeared in April 1995. The first paper in this issue was 'Leadership and Innovation in Universities: from theory to practice', by Burton R. Clark, Allan M. Carter Professor of Higher Education at UCLA; this was one of a series of presentations at EAIR Forums made by Bob Clark, leading to the publication of his seminal work 'Creating Entrepreneurial Universities: organizational pathways of transformation', published in 1998.

In the nine years of TEAM's young life, there have been three significant changes – the journal moved from two to four issues a year in 1997; the publisher changed to Kluwer, the academic publishers in Dordrecht in 1999; and the editorial team expanded. Roddy Begg remains the Editor. He was joined by Barbara Kehm as Co-Editor in 1996, and, later, by Jeroen Huisman, Barbara Sporn and Bjørn Stensaker in 2001. At that point Roddy had 'in-Chief' added to his title and the rest of the 'TEAMteam' were designated 'Editors'.

From the outset the journal has been supported and guided by an Editorial Board of 25 senior practitioners and researchers in the field of higher education, who support the editorial team through the year as reviewers of the Forum presentations (and other papers submitted for publication), and at an annual meeting at the Forum.

EAIR TODAY

These services are important to many of the members, but – for the majority – EAIR remains primarily the provider of an outstanding and unique annual conference where administrators, researchers and policy makers can meet and exchange ideas (and gossip). The conference has visited most of the countries of Europe, and one or two several times. The membership has stabilised at about 600; attendance at the Forum hovered between 250 and 350 for a number of years, but has topped 400 in each of the years in the new Millennium … to an extent that some members feel it is in danger of becoming too big. Feedback (gathered systematically at each of the recent meetings) has confirmed that participants like the basic structure: three days, preferably from Sunday afternoon to Wednesday mid-day ; in late August (northern Europe) or early September (southern Europe); daily plenary keynotes and contributed presentations in six or seven Tracks; presentations in 30 or 40 minute slots; with a couple of social events built into the programme and an optional (more formal) banquet. There have been experiments and innovations, such as posters (to cope with the pressure of there being more promising proposed presentations than available slots) … but the tried and tested basic format seems to be set. EAIR has run the risk of accusations of 'academic tourism' with venues such as a former palace in San Sebastian (Spain), Porto in the year of its being the Cultural Capital of Europe, Berlin at the Millennium … and Prague … but it has resisted the temptation of becoming a hotel based conference and remains institution based, with the academic sessions in a University's regular teaching accommodation, and cheaper accommodation options in the University's student residences … but with 5 star hotels available for those who need the pampered life.

From the beginnings, the Forum has welcomed participants from all continents. The US/Canadian contingent has remained loyal (and includes many of the old stagers who can boast attendance at 10 or more Forums, Charles Bélanger believed to hold the record, 17); the initial dominance of UK and Dutch participation swung towards Scandinavia in the 1990s, but there are now clusters of regulars from Spain and Central and Eastern Europe; each year recently, the Forum Chair has been able to announce participation from over 30 countries worldwide.

As EAIR was conceived and nurtured by AIR, so EAIR itself has seen further sister associations established in Australasia (AAIR), Southern Africa (SAAIR) and South East Asia (SEAAIR). It has welcomed the Executive Director and President of AIR at its Forums and its Chairmen have attended (and been warmly welcomed at) the AIR Forums in May each year. The errant offspring offers a slightly different flavour of participation from its parent. 'Institutional Research' has a different meaning in Europe than the country of EAIR's parentage (as other chapters in this volume will explain). Even today, very few European Universities have Directors (let alone Offices) of Institutional Research … but many have individuals and groups who devote their energies to researching institutional management and governance, a few have (quite substantial) research centres (such as exist in Twente, Kassel and Oslo). In addition, all universities have Rectors/ Presidents/ Vice-Chancellors and Directors of Administration/ Secretaries/ Registrars/ Kanzlers and their staffs, and Ministries of Education their policy officers, and at least some of these office holders take an interest in knowing how the new issues they are tackling – such as massification, internationalisation, diversification etc – have been (or are being) grappled with in other countries. The essence of EAIR is learning from others.

EAIR is unique in Europe, as the 'the' in its title claims, and its adherents often have lonely jobs in their home institutions. They like to huddle together for inspiration (if not for warmth) each year, and - for many members – their EAIR colleagues are more vital to their professional survival than those in their home institutions.

This is how we see it at the Silver Jubilee. We both hope to survive, to have read to us what a new generation (in some cases, still unborn) will feel about EAIR at its Golden Jubilee in 2028!

REFERENCES

Ahrweiler, H. (1979). Welcome Allocution. In C. Cossu (ed.), *Institutional Research in North America and Europe* (pp. 5-7). Paris: Université de Paris 1 (Sorbonne).

Bélanger, C.H. (1979). AIR Internationalism. In C. Cossu (ed.), *Institutional Research in North America and Europe* (p. 89). Paris: Université de Paris 1 (Sorbonne).

Carpentier, P. (1979). The Needs of European Post-secondary Institutions in Institutional Research. In C. Cossu (ed.), *Institutional Research in North America and Europe* (p. 23). Paris: Université de Paris 1 (Sorbonne).

Cossu, C. (1979). *Institutional Research in North America and Europe*. Proceedings of the First EAIR Forum. Paris: Université de Paris 1 (Sorbonne).

Doi, J.I. (1979). The Beginning of a Profession: A Retrospective View. In R. Cope (ed.), *Professional Development for Institutional Research*. New Directions for Institutional Research #23. San Francisco: Jossey-Bass Publishers Inc.

Duggan, A. (1979). The Needs of European Post-secondary Institutions in Institutional Research. In C. Cossu (ed.), *Institutional Research in North America and Europe* (pp. 21-22). Paris: Université de Paris 1 (Sorbonne).

Johnson, F.C. (1979). Curriculum Requirements for Institutional Research. In R. Cope (ed.), *Professional Development for Institutional Research*. New Directions for Institutional Research #23. San Francisco: Jossey-Bass Publishers Inc.

Kail, L. (2003). Personal Correspondence.

Smith, E.R. (1979). An Overview of Planning and Budgeting in North America. In C. Cossu (ed.), *Institutional Research in North America and Europe* (p. 54). Paris: Université de Paris 1 (Sorbonne).

Tetlow, W.L.Jr. (1973). *Institutional Research: The Emergence of a Staff Function in Higher Education*. Unpublished doctoral dissertation, Cornell University, NY.

Tetlow, W.L.Jr. (1979). From History Observed, One May Prophesy. In R. Cope (ed.), *Professional Development for Institutional Research*. New Directions for Institutional Research #23. San Francisco: Jossey-Bass Publishers Inc.

APPENDIX 1

OFFICERS OF EAIR

Distinguished Members
Burton Clark, UCLA, USA (1997)
Kari Hyppönen, University of Turku, Finland (2000)
Leonard Kail, University of Surrey, UK (1994)
Ulrich Teichler, University of Kassel, Germany (2002)

Presidents
Sir William Taylor, Hull University, UK (1990-92)
JanKarel Gevers, University of Amsterdam, The Netherlands (1992-94)
Marianne Bauer, Göteborg University, Sweden (1994-97)
Ulrich Teichler, University of Kassel, Germany (1997-2001)
Guy Neave, International Association of Universities, Paris, France (2001-03)

Chairmen/women
Leonard Kail, University of Surrey, UK (1990-92)
Michael Wright, Napier University, UK (1992-95)
Kari Hyppönen, University of Turku, Finland (1995-2000)
Roddy Begg, University of Aberdeen, UK (2000-01)
Bente Kristensen, Copenhagen Business School, Denmark (2001 to date)

Vice-Chairmen/women
Edgar Frackmann, H-I-S, Hannover, Germany (1990-91)
Marianne Bauer, Göteborg University, Sweden (1991-92)
Kari Hyppönen, University of Turku, Finland (1994-95)
Peter Maassen, CHEPS, Twente University, The Netherlands (1995-98)
Berit Askling, Göteborg University, Sweden (1998-99)
Roddy Begg, University of Aberdeen, UK (1999-2000)
Bente Kristensen, Copenhagen Business School, Denmark (2000-01)
Lee Harvey, University of Central England, UK (2001 to date)

Executive Secretaries
Peter Maassen, CHEPS, Twente University, The Netherlands (1990-95)
Helmut de Rudder, University of Luneburg, Germany (1995-97)

Secretaries
Roddy Begg, University of Aberdeen, UK (1997-99)
Barbara Kehm, HOF Wittenberg, University of Halle, Germany (1999 to date)

Treasurers
Laurence Denonfoux, Université de Lyon 1, France (1990-93)
Anita Ax, Erasmus University of Rotterdam, The Netherlands (1993-2002)
Robert Hoogewijs, University of Ghent, Belgium (2002 to date)

Chairmen of International Subcommittee of AIR
Charles Bélanger, Université de Montreal, Canada (1979-82)
William L. Tetlow, National Center for Higher Education Management Systems,
Colorado, USA (1982-83)
Martha Mayo, Sandy Corporation, Michigan, USA (1983-85)
Poul Bonde, Aarhus Universitet, Denmark (1985-89)

APPENDIX 2
EAIR Forums: 1979 to 2003

Forum	Year	Place and Country	Forum Chair
1st	1979	Paris, France	Claude Cossu, Université de Paris I
2nd	1980	London, United Kingdom	John Calvert, Loughborough University of Technology
3rd	1981	Louvain-la-Neuve, Belgium	Michel Hecquet, Université Catholique de Louvain
4th	1982	Uppsala, Sweden	Thaly Nilsson, Uppsala University
5th	1983	Maastricht, The Netherlands	Peter de Rooij, University of Limburg
6th	1984	Brussels, Belgium	Franz Bingen, Vesalius College, Vrije Universiteit Brussel
7th	1985	Copenhagen, Denmark	Niels Jørgen Hertzum, University of Copenhagen
8th	1986	Loughborough, United Kingdom	John Calvert, Loughborough University of Technology
9th	1987	Enschede, The Netherlands	Frans van Vught, University of Twente, Center for Higher Education Policy Studies (CHEPS)
10th	1988	Bergen, Norway	Edmund Utne, University of Bergen
11th	1989	Trier, Germany	Edgar Frackmann, Hochschul-Informations-System, Hannover
12th	1990	Lyon, France	Laurence Denonfoux, Université Claude Bernard Lyon I
13th	1991	Edinburgh, United Kingdom	Michael Wright, Napier Polytechnic
14th	1992	Brussels, Belgium	Franz Bingen, Vesalius College, Vrije Universiteit Brussel
15th	1993	Turku, Finland	Kari Hyppönen, University of Turku
16th	1994	Amsterdam, The Netherlands	Liesbeth van Welie, Universiteit van Amsterdam
17th	1995	Zürich, Switzerland	Marcel Herbst, ETH Zürich
18th	1996	Budapest, Hungary	Péter Debreczeni, Debreczeni & Associates Consulting
19th	1997	Warwick, United Kingdom	Michael Shattock, University of Warwick
20th	1998	San Sebastian, Spain	José-Ginés Mora, University of Valencia
21st	1999	Lund, Sweden	Karl-Axel Nilsson, Lund University
22nd	2000	Berlin, Germany	Christine Keitel, Freie Universität Berlin
23rd	2001	Porto, Portugal	Daniel Mora, University of Porto
24th	2002	Prague, Czech Republic	Václav Havlíček, Czech Technical University
25th	2003	Limerick, Ireland	Patrick Cashell, University of Limerick

Note: Forum Chairs and institutions are listed as they were at the time.

MARVIN W. PETERSON

INSTITUTIONAL RESEARCH AND MANAGEMENT IN THE U.S. AND EUROPE: SOME EAIR - AIR COMPARISONS

Abstract. This chapter examines the external conditions that have influenced higher education management in the U.S. and shaped the development of practice of institutional research; compares the status of AIR and EAIR at the anniversary of their 25th Forums; and examines some common external conditions that are currently shaping management and institutional research in the U.S. and Europe. Drawing on the current conditions and the experience of AIR since its 25th Anniversary, some concluding comments suggest a more pro-active role for EAIR in shaping management and policy analysis in Europe

INTRODUCTION

Being invited to write a chapter on institutional research and management in the U.S. for this special publication on the 25th anniversary of EAIR is for me both a personal irony and an intriguing challenge. The personal irony is that I was president of AIR during the anniversary year of its 25th Annual Forum (Portland, Oregon, May 1985) and now, almost two decades later, I have the opportunity to contribute to EAIR's 25th Annual Forum celebration. The reality, of course, is that I had served on AIR's board when the question of whether and how to include an international focus to our U.S. efforts was being debated, was present when efforts to ensure European representation on the AIR Board was effectively thwarted by an AIR By-law change which required all Board members to be elected at large, was involved in discussions with several EAIR founding members about this new association and have continued to be an active participant in both AIR and EAIR Annual Forums for the past two decades. But then the irony may be no more than longevity!

The intriguing challenge is to determine how to discuss institutional research and management in the U.S. in a way that contributes to EAIR's celebration of its first 25 years. Clearly one could examine the development of the two associations, AIR and EAIR, and their changing relationship. That, however, is best reserved for a more systematic, comparative effort - perhaps including other groups like the Australasian AIR. Another approach would be to examine the development of the field of institutional research - comparing and contrasting the North American and European perspectives. That probably is beyond the scope of a brief chapter such as this.

Rather my intent is to examine the evolution of institutional research in the U.S. from a contingency perspective, to see how AIR has evolved and to speculate on its implications for EAIR. A contingency perspective suggests that external conditions have largely shaped the primary management challenges and performance demands that colleges and universities in the U.S. have had to address. The practice of institutional research, I suggest, has evolved primarily as a response to, or in anticipation of, these challenges and demands on our institutions. In turn AIR has developed as an

R. Begg (ed.), The Dialogue between Higher Education Research and Practice, 31–44.
© 2003 *Kluwer Academic Publishers. Printed in the Netherlands.*

association that has attempted to interpret the nature of the emerging field as a profession and to respond to the needs of its members.

Although this chapter focuses primarily on institutional research and management in the U.S., it is suggested that such a contingency analysis may be useful in understanding and interpreting the evolution of IR in the European context and may account for differences as well as similarities in AIR and EAIR. The chapter is divided into four sections. The first examines how external conditions have exerted management and performance pressures on institutions in the U.S., which in turn have shaped the practice and the profession of institutional research. The second section provides a brief contrast of AIR and EAIR on their 25th anniversary and suggests how U.S. and European conditions may explain some of their similarities and differences. The third discusses a set of emerging conditions that institutions in both the U.S. and Europe must address that may change our practice of institutional research. Finally, some observations on the implications of these emerging conditions and the recent experience of AIR for EAIR are offered.

A CONTINGENCY PERSPECTIVE: IR AND MANAGEMENT IN THE U.S.

Institutional research, as a set of organised institutional activities and practices, were identified in the U.S. much earlier than in Europe. Although institutional research activities and practices were identified prior to World War II, institutional research, as a formally organised function in the U.S., emerged in the 1950s (Cowley 1959; Brumbaugh 1960). An invited gathering of 46 concerned individuals met in 1961 in Chicago (This was later identified as the first Forum even though AIR was not founded until 1964). This meeting and papers it generated marked the start of a rapid period of growth of both the practice of institutional research and of the field as a profession.

1950s and 60s Growth, Expansion and Emergence of IR

The post World War II era in the U.S. was marked by an unprecedented period of growth and expansion in U.S. higher education. Strong public support for higher education, governmental commitment and funding and enrolment demands increased the size, number and type of institutions, especially in the public sector. Pressure on institutional management during this period of rapid expansion demanded a rationale for their institution's direction and for data to account for the students they were serving, the faculty they needed, and financial and facilities resources they were requesting. Institutional performance meant becoming more accountable for resources. Institutional research activities focused on data collection, on developing data definitions and information systems and on quantitative, descriptive analyses of enrolment, space utilisation, costs, student and faculty characteristics and examining various self-study issues. AIR in its early years assisted practitioners in discovering their own peers, sharing problems and comparing approaches. Members also examined and debated the nature and role of the emerging profession - the theory vs. practice focus of their work; the need for an independent perspective vs. serving management, etc. Association activities included expanding membership, developing the Annual Forum, publishing a Newsletter and Directory and some special publications.

1965 - 1975 Disruption, Control and Professionalism

In the late 1960s and early 1970s higher education was attacked both from within and without. Large impersonal institutions, increasingly professional faculty and critical students were a source of internal stress and dissatisfaction. External issues such as the Vietnam War, civil rights and the free speech movement found fertile ground and led to major disruptions on many campuses. The management pressure was for control and order on campus and to assure greater access for non-traditional and minority students – two pressures that often served to further fuel campus disruptions. To assure the public that disruptions were not undermining the quality of educational effort, comparative and reputational studies promoted initially by prestigious groups like the American Council on Education (ACE) also became a focus of institutional research efforts. Studies of campus and programme quality and reputation, on the correlates of quality, and an expanded interest in student behaviour and attitudes were common. Enhancing the capacity of institutions to publicly report such results were also emphasised. During this period AIR gave greater attention to examining controversial issues, to promoting the use of new research methods (survey, qualitative, etc.) and to establishing a central office to better serve the association's growing membership and to reflect the increasingly quasi-professional nature of the field.

1975 - 1985 Recession, Efficiency and Results

Beginning in the mid 1970s and extending into the 1980s, higher education was subjected to a major economic recession in the U.S., which coincided with the end of the Post World War II baby boom. Both enrolments and financial support stagnated and forecasts for the next decade offered little reassurance. The resulting pressure on management again changed. On the one hand institutions were pressed to become more efficient and at the same time become more market oriented since enrolments could no longer be supplemented by seeking new applicant groups. The impact of the 1972 Higher Education Amendments, which gave financial aid directly to students (not to institutions) made the market for students even more competitive. This new reality stressed performance based on results - not just inputs or resources used. Management emphasis began to focus on strategic planning and reduction and reallocation approaches. The impact of this was clearly reflected in institutional research. Emphasis on quantitative productivity and efficiency studies, evaluative research and varied forecasting, budgeting and planning studies (Fincher 1985) increased. This was also the period in which extensive use of computers in the development of management information systems and in conducting institutional research was expanding rapidly. Some even argued that institutional researchers should become telematics technologists (Sheehan 1985).

An Interlude: EAIR and AIR's 25th Anniversary Perspective

In the context of EAIR's current celebration, it is useful to look at the development of the field of institutional research in the U.S. and at the state of AIR at the time of its 25th Anniversary Forum. Clearly by 1985 institutional research in the U.S. was a well-developed field of practice and widely recognised as an important institutional management function. Most campuses had an institutional research office. Membership in AIR had grown steadily. The Annual Forum was a well-run conference and the association had a national headquarters located at Florida State University with an administrative director and a small staff. Regional associations had been formed but with varying degrees of success. AIR publications now included the NDIR series published jointly with Jossey–Bass publishers, the Research in Higher Education Journal, the Professional File Series and occasional special monographs. The debate over AIR's international role and attempts to provide greater European involvement on the AIR board and its policy and programme content had been recently resolved with the establishment of EAIR as a separate sister association in Europe. By all measures, institutional research in the U.S. was a well-established set of institutional practices, was recognised as an administrative function, and had its own professional association.

However, the future in 1984–85 was not altogether optimistic. Partially as a result of the economic recession, membership and attendance at the Annual Forum had declined for two successive years. Many were concerned that the 'office of institutional research' no longer reported to the president (or executive vice president) and did not 'control' all the institutional studies on campus. Some argued it was losing status and possibly legitimacy. Computerisation and large-scale databases were making information more widely available within institutions. The advent of micro computing and widespread access to information was proliferating the research being done on many campuses in an uncontrolled fashion. The period was labeled in one analysis as one of 'fragmentation and uncertainty' (Peterson 1985).

During the year leading up to the 25th AIR Annual Forum (in May, 1985), the Board of AIR decided to focus that year's Forum on an assessment of the field and to establish a planning committee to chart the direction of the association. One result was an NDIR Volume, Institutional Research in Transition (Corcoran & Peterson 1985), which captured the emerging and changing nature of the field, identified the forces reshaping it, suggested an agenda for further developing the field as a profession, and advocated a more proactive, transformational role for the association in promoting that development.

As a first step, in 1984-85 AIR broadened its mission so that it focused on institutional research as an 'inclusive process of information collection, analysis, research and utilization related to planning, management, resource allocation and evaluation decisions'. It was no longer just as an office with a set of activities. The following year the AIR Planning Task Force chaired by Marilyn McCoy adopted a strategy for the association designed to move the field forward. Since 1984-85 AIR has continued to grow, to expand its membership and professional services and, periodically, returned to reassess and to revise its plan. AIR changed from a responsive association to a more proactive one.

1985 - 1995 Quality, Planning and Assessment

By the mid 1980s the management focus on improved efficiency and marketing was no longer sufficient to deal with realities. The economic constraints of the early 1980s were now seen as long term. A period of reduction, reallocation and retrenchment was foreseen. Even the booming economy of the early 1990s only temporarily eased the financial constraints as institutions looked increasingly to tuition and private resources.

Demographic shifts now reflected real declines in traditional age students and new markets of ethnically, educationally or economically deprived students were limited. Many of these either could not afford higher education or needed special programmes. Proprietary institutions now competed more effectively for students. Numerous other not for profit service organisations competed for the private resources. The period of reduction, reallocation, retrenchment and strategic planning was not sufficient. Management pressures began to call for real institutional change.

The mid 1980s also introduced another curious twist in this era of constraints and change. In 1994 a U.S. Office of Education sponsored study Group on Conditions of Excellence in American Higher Education published its report on <u>Involvement in Learning</u> (1994). This report criticised the uneven quality of undergraduate education in the U.S. and challenged colleges and universities to increase student expectations, to promote active learning strategies and to measure educational and instructional quality and to use assessment of student learning outcomes. The Quality Improvement movement from business and industry gained a foothold in higher education and found a substantial following among public policy leaders, accreditation associations and some institutional leaders.

Clearly this was a decade that challenged institutional leaders to examine their institutional purposes to deal with resource limitations and to address issues of educational quality and institutional effectiveness. The performance focus on results shifted from quantitative measures of efficiency in the previous decade to measures of institutional effectiveness, educational quality and student outcomes and learning while also considering restructuring their institutions.

In this milieu institutional research has been challenged and has expanded its repertoire of studies and techniques as never before. Planning and policy analysis studies to support institutional change, increased use of comparative cross and institutional analysis to justify existing and new programmes, awareness and use of external data reflecting environment forces on higher education, and extensive development of student assessment systems and measures all became major areas of institutional research effort. At the association level these are reflected in Forum related workshops and national institutes dealing with qualitative as well as quantitative methods, in a new Annual Forum Track on student assessment and in research grants and training programmes to enhance institutional researchers capacity to use national databases for comparative research in their own campus studies. AIR now has begun obtaining grants to support its professional development initiatives and partnering with other associations in some of its programme initiatives.

Beyond 25: AIR Today

Clearly much has changed in the field of institutional research and in AIR since the 25th Anniversary Forum in 1985. This largely reflects the dynamism of the field of institutional research and the more proactive nature of AIR.

The field of institutional research is now understood in terms of AIR's decision in 1984 to adopt a broader mission that focuses on the process of data collection, analysis and use for institutional decisions. This broadened focus allowed the field to continue to incorporate new types of data and analysis techniques that served the new management challenges that institutions face. It has also led to a membership that includes administrators, analysts and researchers not found in offices bearing the traditional institutional research name or that reflects institutional research offices that have added staff that reflect new analytic and data management needs.

AIR also has changed. An Executive Director with strong research and analysis skills now heads the central office. The Annual Forum includes new tracks including one on assessment. The association sponsors week-long institutes designed to provide professional development in important areas of institutional research. The association now seeks government and association grants to provide further training and to assist its members. The association has become active in trying to influence government data collection policies and practices. And the association is actively working with other associations - both those affiliated with institutional research and some representing other higher education academic or administrative groups.

Clearly the period after the 25th Forum in Portland has witnessed a field that has responded to management challenges that reflect the changing world of higher education. It also reflects an association, AIR, that continues to be proactive-working to transform the field of practice.

EAIR AND AIR AT TWENTY FIVE

Having examined the evolution of institutional research and AIR in the U.S. as a product of or contingent upon the external conditions, which exert management pressures on the institution, one is tempted to conduct a similar analysis in European context. However, that is probably best left to one of my EAIR colleagues. What may be more useful for the purposes of this volume is to compare/contrast EAIR and AIR and to ask a more direct question. At a comparable point in time (their 25th Forum), are the two associations more similar or different? And if so, why?

In doing so I should apologise since this is primarily a comparison based on limited observations at EAIR and AIR Forums, conversations with EAIR colleagues, participation in earlier discussions regarding AIR's international interest and planning of EAIR, and familiarity with the TEAM. This clearly is impressionistic and non-systematic. Perhaps it will motivate one of my EAIR colleagues to do a careful history and contingency analysis of the development of EAIR.

The Associations: Structure

EAIR like AIR started with a small group of individuals with a desire to meet with like-minded associates. The difference, of course, is that in the case of AIR a major national presidential association (the American Council on Education) helped promote the initial meetings while in EAIR's situation they started with a small group of AIR attendees who eventually realised a separate organisation in a European setting was more desirable: one where they could be represented and influence the directions of the association, could insure a more relevant set of topics and could attract greater European attendance.

Both organisations began with a campus-based office with association business handled on a voluntary basis by one of their members. However, by their 25th

Anniversary both had evolved to an office with a full time administrator and a small staff.

Annual Forum

After 25 years EAIR's Annual Forum is less than half the size of AIR's at a comparable time. But given the variation among nations represented and the economic and logistical constraints, this is probably not significant. The level of programme complexity of EAIR's Forum - themes, major speakers, types of sessions and range of topics etc. - is not unlike AIR in the mid 1980s - (except, of course, for the European tradition of meeting on campus - which AIR also did before it became too large).

Publications

EAIR like AIR has sought to both legitimise the profession, to inform its members and to promote emerging topics and issues by publishing its own journal, TEAM. Although AIR had more vehicles for member exchange (Professional File, NDIR, etc.) by their 25th Anniversary, most were in the early stages of development.

Membership

Although this does not reflect a careful analysis of membership, EAIR appears to have a somewhat different membership group. Particularly noteworthy is the fact that a seemingly greater portion of EAIR members are mid to upper level administrators, policy analysts from government agencies and scholars than AIR. (Although AIR used to have more senior members than today!) EAIR's attendees are also older - perhaps reflecting the more limited access to travel funds in Europe and the larger, more varied offices that employ more junior members in the U.S.

This, perhaps, reflects one of the most significant differences between EAIR and AIR. AIR is an association of institutional researchers and analysts - including many junior staff people. EAIR is more an association of managers, administrators or governmental policy analysts. This, no doubt, reflects the European context where in the recent past, institutional level administration was less developed and is still being expanded.

Content

Probably reflecting the membership characteristics, the content focus of EAIR - its Annual Forum sessions, TEAM articles, etc. - seems to be more on managerial and policy issues. Whereas AIR, even in 1985, was focused to a greater degree on specific institutional studies, methods and techniques of research and on information technology and its applications. In addition to member differences this probably also reflects the extensive national contextual differences. For example, 25 years ago many European nations were highly centralised national systems. In the interim, most have been dealing with issues of decentralisation and deregulation of their centralised systems and on building institutional management capacity. Also, the emergence of the

EU and the various attempts to harmonise very different systems, institutions and educational programmes has placed a priority on the policy and managerial issues that these dynamics require. Thus, institutional leaders had to deal with broad management issues. In the U.S. differences among states are not as extreme and institutional research demands are not influenced as extensively by attempts to decentralise state systems or to coordinate and integrate systems or policies in different states.

Professional Development

Clearly all professional associations, AIR and EAIR included, are concerned with the professional development, which helps their members to perform at their highest capability and assures that new and emerging approaches and techniques are incorporated into their professional field. Both AIR and EAIR at their 25th Anniversary were attempting to do this through their publications and the topics addressed in their Annual Forum. However, many professional development efforts also occur through special workshops or larger institutes designed to inform and teach. At its 25th Anniversary AIR was only beginning to use pre-Forum workshops; EAIR still has not been extensively involved in such efforts. Professional development activities, of course, have been a major focus of AIR recently - sponsoring numerous pre-Forum workshops, holding national training institutes and cooperating with other associations to promote such efforts.

Summary: A 25th Anniversary Comparison

Comparing EAIR and AIR at the time of their 25th Forum can be summarised in terms of form, content and style. In form EAIR has developed as an organisation that is structurally very similar to AIR - just not as large. Both offer the same type of professional activities - Annual Forum, publications and some member services, although AIR's are more numerous. Content reflects more differences most apparent is that EAIR is a more managerial and policy oriented association while AIR is more oriented towards institutional studies, research methods and techniques. As noted previously, this may reflect the context of institutions which are emerging from national systems in Europe and whose administrative, managerial and policy staff are historically much different than the states in the U.S.

Of course one cannot overlook the differences in style between EAIR and AIR. AIR and its various activities, while catering to members from various states, systems, institutional types and analytic roles, are still not as culturally rich and differentiated as EAIR's members who represent different nations and a far more unique set of cultures.

INTO THE LOOKING GLASS:
SIMILAR OR DIFFERENT FUTURES

In the U.S. clearly institutional research has evolved as an analytic response to institutions managerial challenges and the external conditions they faced. EAIR, while reflecting a structural form and set of activities that are similar to those of AIR at its 25th Anniversary, differs significantly in its content and style. Despite these differences, one question of interest is how institutional research will change as new external conditions arise and new managerial challenges emerge. This section identifies seven conditions (Peterson 1999) that institutions are now facing in the U.S. and Europe and asks: whether these are the same in the U.S. and Europe? and what the implications for management and for institutional research on our two continents are?

Changing Patterns of Access and Diversity

Although access to higher education has reached a very high level in the U.S., pressure to maintain it and increase it for some undeserved groups is likely to continue. In Europe while the level of participation in higher education differs extensively by country - especially with the inclusion of many new Eastern European countries - increasing access remains and will continue to be an important pressure on higher education both politically for its contribution to economic development and socially to respond to the growing demands for and interest in it.

Closely related to the issue of access is the diversity of enrolment. In the U.S. this pursuit primarily reflects our concern for disadvantaged ethnic minority groups - Hispanic, Black, certain Asian groups and Native Americans - and is unlikely to abate. In Europe the issue is less clearly defined as particular groups seeking greater access and opportunity for higher education will differ by country. However, it often reflects issues of either lack of access for lower economic groups or access for ethnic minority groups who have immigrated in large numbers. These patterns of immigration may reflect the influx from former colonies or groups attracted to fill employment needs of a country. More importantly the emergence of the European Union and the stress on promoting cross-national enrolment assures that institutions in most European countries will be serving a culturally or linguistically more diverse student body for this reason as well.

The issues of access and diversity carry a critical academic management challenge for higher education in both the U.S. and Europe to respond with new admissions, student support and academic programmes to serve increasing numbers of more diverse students. The challenge for institutional research is to anticipate the issues raised, to access the characteristics, needs and performance of these students and to evaluate the institutional responses to them.

The Telematics Revolution

One does not need to describe the extensive impact of the expansion of the interaction of information systems, computing capacity and telecommunications technology on higher education's academic and administrative processes. This pervades institutions in both the U.S. and Europe and is changing both our internal systems of administration, teaching and learning and our external capacity to deliver educational material and learning experiences in new modes of distance education. Although this revolution may not overwhelm higher education as rapidly and pervasively as its proponents forecast during the past decade, it seems clear that advances in these interactive technologies and our understanding of how to use them will continue to be a major pressure for change in the next decade.

The challenges for management - especially in the academic applications - require addressing issues of how to evaluate the potential of new technologies, how to acquire and maintain them, how to use them most effectively by revising existing academic programmes and providing training and support for both faculty and students in their use as teaching-learning devises, how to design new distance education networks including consideration of corporate partnerships with other higher educational institutions and with information resource, computer, telecommunications and entertainment organisations who often control the development and application of the technologies. Clearly institutional research is one institutional function that needs to understand these new technologies, to be able to assess their potential applications, to evaluate faculty and student competence in using them for teaching and learning, to assess the educational impact and value for student learning and even, to examine new strategic arrangements for introducing these technologies, distance education strategies and new institutional partnerships.

Academic Quality and Institutional Effectiveness

The concern for educational quality and institutional effectiveness arose as an issue in the 1990s, not only in the U.S., but also throughout Europe. While most of the focus in the U.S. has been on student assessment as a response to critical national reports on student learning and performance at both the K-12 and higher education level, the focus in Europe has been more on programme quality of academic and research units. This often reflected government's attempts to ensure institutional accountability and performance as they moved towards deregulation and decentralisation of their national system. (One should note that programme review was widely adopted by many states in the U.S. before student assessment became popular). Given the increasing public interest in and demand for higher education amidst rising political concerns about the costs and contribution of higher education to economic productivity, it is unlikely that concerns about academic quality and the best means for assuring it will abate in either Europe or the U.S. One should note that Europe has a further complication as it tries to address issues of common academic credit among institutions from very different systems and countries. At least the U.S. has long history of the Carnegie Course Credit (despite its many critics) and government programme classifications to use in cross-institutional transfer and comparisons.

The challenge to academic administrators is both an institutional and a political one. Externally they have to address highly political concerns about the meaning of quality and effectiveness as well as to design approaches to evaluate and accredit programmes and institutions. Internally they have to develop approaches to evaluating the quality or effectiveness (not just the efficiency) of academic programmes, of new modes of delivery, of faculty teaching efforts and of student performance or learning. The challenge for institutional research in this arena is no longer a simple one of examining quantitative indicators of educational productivity and efficiency. Institutional research must now examine the external political dynamics and consequences of different meanings of quality and effectiveness and of means for accessing it, while dealing with difficult internal issues of faculty, of academic programme or discipline and individual student measures of these constructs. More importantly, they need to be engaged in developing measures for them and processes for evaluating programmes and teaching and learning strategies.

The Rise of Economic Productivity

Both the U.S. and Europe have had a long history of assuming higher education was an important contributor to economic development through our research and our education of students for governmental, professional and technical leadership positions. "Knowledge development" and 'knowledge transfer" were two well understood functions of higher education that the U.S. and most European countries accepted as their primary mode of contributing to economic development - we just had different approaches to organising our systems (free enterprise vs. planned). However, the growing awareness of the contributions of higher education to individuals and indirectly to society's well-being, of the increase of international transferability of knowledge and highly trained individuals, of the role of applied research and training to economic improvement, and of the rise of global markets in which advanced economies were supported by strong higher education systems, has led to an increasing awareness of a more complex view of higher education's role in economic development. Institutions are now seen as applied and policy research centres, continuing professional education centres, sites of research parks, as incubators of new businesses and even partners with business and government in developing regional economic development strategies. Higher educational institutions are increasingly key players in regional and national economic development and play roles that go well beyond being the traditional provider of advancing knowledge and training educated personnel.

The challenges to institutional leaders, as this new mode of economic development has emerged, requires understanding this new institutional role and the external business and government groups with whom they must work; creating new on-campus units to participate; linking the new applied research, training and strategy roles with more traditional faculty teaching and research roles; and guiding and directing units that may be funded and managed very differently from traditional academic units. Institutional researchers response to this management challenge requires far greater awareness of economic, business, and employment data and analyses, the ability to conduct strategic analyses of new functions and even organisational arrangements; and working with government policy analysts and business strategy analysts.

Relearning Markets

One of the impacts of greater access to higher education and engaging in a more aggressive economic development mode in highly competitive countries and a global world is the realisation that the need for postsecondary education does not end with a degree, nor perhaps does higher education's obligation. Citizens who failed to get a college education may belatedly see its value, companies undergoing changes in their competitive environment may need employees with new skills, college graduates may change fields. These markets for postsecondary education and relearning are, even in advanced nations like the U.S. and Europe, often far larger than the existing college age cohort. Both the need for postsecondary education and the demand for it by these groups are increasingly being delivered by non-educational organisations as well as by colleges and universities and are being recognised by political analysts as an important postsecondary educational arena.

Institutional leaders addressing this postsecondary relearning market faces management challenges in identifying them, in designing and implementing programmes to serve them and in understanding the patterns of demand, financing and competition in this ill defined, often fluid, market. Institutional research again faces the challenges of assisting management in analysing these market patterns and assessing the performance of less traditional academic programmes and delivery systems designed to reach them.

Globalisation

Perhaps one of the most overused and ill-defined terms in discussing the conditions impacting higher education is globalisation. The concept, broadly defined as adopting a perspective beyond one's own nation, is often used in higher education to discuss faculty and student exchanges, study of foreign language and culture, or introducing "global perspectives" in our curriculum. But increasingly it also includes international networks of scholars, government analysts and/or corporate researchers; topics of global focus (global warming, hunger, etc); or even networks of institutions designed to support global research efforts or educational opportunities. The phenomenon is both extensive and ill defined yet one, that is expanding rapidly and relevant in both the U.S. and Europe.

The management challenge to higher education is how to become aware of this emerging pattern of higher education research and teaching that is organised or delivered in a global form and knowing how to engage their own institutions or its members in such arrangements. Once again the role of institutional researchers is one of exploration - identifying various patterns of globalisation, tracking them as well as their own institution's pattern of participation and examining the impact.

Cost Constraint

A final reality is recognising that even in advanced countries with relatively wealthy economies, the rising costs of higher education are a significant constraint in both Europe and the U.S. Despite the advantage of well-developed institutions of higher education, most of our countries have many other demands on public funding. Higher education, while valued, will not be the likely recipient of extensive new sources of funding to respond to all the external conditions and management challenges already identified. The management challenge, for the foreseeable future, will still require simultaneous sensitivity to revenues, resources and results - and institutional research will have to provide analyses that recognise these three "R's".

SOME IMPLICATIONS FOR EAIR

At the 25th Anniversary of the EAIR Forum, it appears to have followed a similar pattern of development to AIR in its first 25 years. They both had a similar organisational structure - a campus based office with an administrative director; were focused on responding to the needs of their members; and had a similar set of activities - primarily a Forum, a journal and emerging publication efforts. However, they differed somewhat in their membership and in conduct of their primary activities. AIR's members were primarily institutional researchers and oriented to analysing campus-based management issues and institutional research methods and techniques. EAIR's membership was comprised more of institutional and governmental administrators and policy analysts and were more management and policy oriented. This, no doubt, reflects the fact that European institutions were changing their national systems and were in the process of deregulating and decentralising their systems and still building institutional level management teams. In effect this difference in membership, content focus and management vs. institutional research orientation probably suggests the wisdom of forming two separate and somewhat distinctive associations.

However, AIR's history in the two decades since their 25th Forum Anniversary and the similarities in external conditions and management challenges now faced in both the U.S. and Europe may provide some insight for EAIR as it embarks on its second twenty-five years.

A major shift in AIR after its 25th Anniversary was its redirection from an association that primarily served its membership needs to one that also became more proactive in shaping the development of the field of institutional research and advocating for it. Rather than merely coordinating the Annual Forum for member exchange and publishing a journal, Research in Higher Education, for the exchange of papers, it began the Professional File which educated members in the use of techniques and methods, sponsored the NDIR series which captured major developments, and co-sponsored Higher Education: The Handbook of Theory and Research which provided an in-depth theoretical and research based examination on issues in higher education. These efforts were designed to advance the field of institutional research, as were their special publications.

AIR also began to address more seriously the role of educating institutional researchers. An extensive array of workshops prior to the Annual Forum now provides training on specific topics or methods. They also sponsor two major institutes - one on institutional research as a field and one on information systems and methods. The educational role extends to attempt to promote graduate training in the field by encouraging graduate student participation in their various events and providing special incentives and opportunities for graduate student participation.

AIR has also seriously begun to represent the field more broadly to government and to other professional associations. Recent co-sponsorship of a national data institute with the national Center for Educational Statistics and the National Science Foundation has served to strengthen the relationship of AIR with these national data collection efforts and to promote the use of such data by institutional researchers and higher education researchers. Other efforts include co-sponsorship of special topic conferences with other associations such as the Council for the Advancement and Support of Education, the Association for the Study of Higher Education and the Society for College and University Planning among others.

While AIR and EAIR share a common history and strong bond, there is clearly a difference in the membership and primary focus - EAIR is more management and policy focused and probably appropriately so in the European context. However, the commonality of issues they face suggests topical areas for joint future work. Also AIR's decision to move beyond merely serving its members to promoting the development of the field and to represent it to government and to other associations may suggest a possible new direction on strategy for EAIR in promoting management and policy analysis in Europe. Some strategies might include:

1. Actively promoting the development of management and policy analysis as a professional field and administrative function.
2. Developing more in service educational or training efforts for both new members and for advanced members.
3. Focusing on European Union issues and problems and, where possible, advocating particular approaches and changes.
4. Encouraging the development of university based programmes (certificates or degrees) in higher education management and policy analysis. (Europe lacks the strong array of higher education graduate degree programmes that are present in the U.S.).

It goes without saying that pursuing a proactive agenda, to make management and policy analysis as visible in Europe as institutional research is in the U.S., is an ambitious one. It may be timely, but it would, no doubt, require strengthening EAIR's central office, adding more professional staff leadership and finding financial support beyond just member dues.

REFERENCES

Brumbaugh, A.J. (1960). *Research Designed to Improve Institutions of Higher Learning*. Washington, DC, American Council on Education.

Cowley, W.H. (1959). Two and a Half Centuries of Institutional Research. In R.G. Axt and H.T. Sprague (Eds.), *College Self Study: Lectures on Institutional Research*. Boulder, CO., Western Institute Commission on Higher Education.

Fincher, C. (1985). The Art of Science of Institutional Research, in M. Corcoran and M. Peterson (eds.), *Institutional Research in Transition*. NDIR, Vol. 46. San Francisco, CA. Jossey-Bass.

Peterson, M.W. (1999). The Role of Institutional Research: From Improvement to Redesign. In V.F. Volkwein (ed.) *What is Institutional Research all About?* NDIR, No. 104. San Francisco, CA: Jossey-Bass,.

Sheehan, B.S. (1985). Telematics and Decision Support Intermediary. In M. Corcoran and M. Peterson (eds). *Institutional Research in Transition*. NDIR, No. 46. San Francisco, CA: Jossey-Bass.

PART 2

RESEARCH AND PRACTICE

ULRICH TEICHLER

HIGHER EDUCATION RESEARCH IN EUROPE

Abstract. Though higher education research has grown substantially over the last three or four decades, it is still conceived as a relatively small and vulnerable field of research. Higher education research both gains and suffers from the fact that there are no clear borderlines between higher educational researchers and other higher education "experts". Academic research on higher education has gained some visibility and identity in Europe, while persons conducting research on higher education being associated to governments, umbrella organisations or administration of individual higher education institutions are hardly visible, although their number exceeds that of the academic higher education resarchers.

EAIR, as the only visible body in Europe exclusively focussing on the role to provide fora for the communication among different types of higher education experts, helps to disseminate the achievements of higher educational research and to encourage policymakers and practitioners to be involved actively in research. In the future, EAIR could pay more attention to the growing numbers of higher educational professionals and to their interest in getting involved in higher education research.

INTRODUCTION

In the 1970s, when EAIR was founded, higher education was a relatively small field of research. In the meantime, higher education research has grown substantially. We note various associations and agencies involved in promoting research on higher education or other kinds of systematic information gathering on higher education. Several journals are available publishing, exclusively or among others, academic articles on higher education. Obviously, the interest among practitioners in the findings of higher education research has increased significantly. Finally, there is a more sizeable number of persons whose prime professional activity is to undertake higher education research than of persons involved in higher education research activities as part of their professional activities.

The notion is widespread in Europe that higher education research has not yet become a fairly stable field; we often describe higher education as a fragmented field of research. This notion of a research field still being in the process of getting eventually stable and mature is not merely a matter of size. Certainly, most observers would estimate that the number of fulltime higher education researchers in Europe is less than 1,000 and that the number of other persons involved in systematic information gathering in higher education is at most in the range of a few thousands. But other factors come into play as well. International comparison suggests that research on higher education in Europe remained a relatively smaller field of research than notably in the United States of America as well as in Australia, China and formerly in the Soviet Union (cf. Sadlak and Altbach 1997).

Therefore, we might conclude this essay at once, on the very first page, deplore the state of affairs and formulate good wishes for a brighter future. However, if we look at the state of higher education research more closely, we note that the strength and the weakness of higher education research rests both in the fact that higher education research is not a clearly defined and segmented area in its own right, but rather might be viewed as a fuzzy entity among many more or less systematic information gathering and reflective exercises on higher education. This essay, thus, aims to look at higher

47

R. Begg (ed.), The Dialogue between Higher Education Research and Practice, 47–54.
© 2003 *Kluwer Academic Publishers. Printed in the Netherlands.*

education research both as a specific entity and as a part of a wider range of systematic data gathering and reflection.

CHARACTERISTICS OF HIGHER EDUCATION RESEARCH

One way to understand the character of higher education research is to compare it to the areas of research which we tend to consider as the most prototypical ones. This certainly leads us to the conclusion that four characteristics of higher education research can be pointed out as distinct from what we consider the mainstream of research. These characteristics do not merely apply to higher education research in Europe, but rather to this domain worldwide.

First, higher education is an interdisciplinary field of research. The theme 'higher education' can be analysed with the help of various disciplines, e.g. pedagogy, psychology, sociology, political science, economics and business studies, law and history (cf. also Becher 1992). A broad range of phenomena and abstractions of the real world of higher education are the focus of research, and most of these phenomena are too complex to be addressed by a single discipline; often, various disciplines and various methods come into play. As it is true for others areas of interdisciplinary research also, higher education research often is undertaken by researchers who consider themselves embedded in a certain discipline and understand higher education as one of the thematic areas they just happen to give preference to in their research activities for a limited time-span of their career. Therefore, the number of scholars interacting and cooperating under the label of 'higher education research' is even smaller than one would expect from observing the available academic literature.

Second, research on higher education shares the fate with most interdisciplinary research of having a more vulnerable institutional basis than disciplinary research (see Schwarz and Teichler 2000). In most universities of the world, disciplinary structures dominate and are reinforced by the departmental divides. Interdisciplinary research is often based on informal modes of cross-cutting cooperation or is accommodated in special research units which often are viewed as non-permanent entities of a university. Eventually, however, the view spread in the 1990s that research organised according to themes and research aiming to be relevant gradually gets on a par with the disciplinary-based pursuit of knowledge for its own sake (see Gibbons et al. 1995).

Third, research on higher education altogether has to be 'strategic'. It has to contribute both to the tasks of basic research, i.e. enhancing theory, methodology and basic understanding of the theme irrespective of the possible use of the knowledge acquired, and to the tasks of applied knowledge, i.e. providing systematic knowledge which could immediately be useful to practical problem-solving. However, most individual researchers do not cover by themselves this broad span of theoretical and practical emphasis. Rather, higher education research is very heterogeneous in this respect.

Fourth, higher education research analyses an area in which most of the actors are highly trained and knowledgeable in their professional domain. As the consequence, there are no clear borderlines betw   1 the researchers and the reflective actors, and many actors believe that they do not need any specialised research in order to understand and eventually improve their domain of action (cf. Teichler 1996).

These conditions might be deplored as too fuzzy and too heterogeneous, but they can be viewed as well as an exciting challenge. Higher education research can draw from a multitude of disciplines, theories and methods and can incorporate the knowledge and experiences of scholars and actors of the higher education system. It can both contribute to the improvement of the body of knowledge and to actors' reflections and actual changes in the higher education system.

FRAGMENTATION OF RESEARCH ACCORDING TO ACTORS AND FUNCTIONS?

In the framework of the conference which aimed to analyse the relationships between higher education research and the actors in the higher education system (Teichler and Sadlak 2000), the U.S. American higher education researcher Elaine El-Khawas (2000) pointed out that higher education research is fragmented according to three separate bases: 'research, policy and practice':
- 'Research' understood as higher education research based in academic units of universities. Many education schools at U.S. universities offer masters and doctoral programmes in higher education; thus, academic research on higher education had a backbone in the position of professors serving these programmes.
- 'Policy' in terms of research activities and units within or closely linked to supra-institutional actors in higher education, e.g. governments and related agencies as well as umbrella organisations of higher education.
- 'Practice' understood as research directly linked to the administration of higher education institutions. A substantial number of universities in the U.S. have established a unit of 'institutional research' which undertakes analyses at the request of the university administration in order to provide the information base considered necessary for improvement of the higher education institution.

This situation is by no means new. It emerged in the 1960s and 1970s when higher education in the U.S. expanded substantially; higher education management made a leap forward towards professionalisation and higher education research developed towards a visible field of research. During that period, the Association for Institutional Research (AIR) was founded as an association primarily serving the interaction of applied higher education researchers linked to the university administration, i.e. the researcher in the domain 'practice' in El-Khawas' terminology. And the Association for the Study of Higher Education (ASHE) was founded in the late 1970s as an association of the academics active in higher education, i.e. the scholars in the domain of 'research' according to El-Khawas.

In the late 1970s, members of AIR succeeded in encouraging Europeans to start a series of conferences and to form an association which, in 1989, became 'EAIR'. The survival and long-term success of EAIR certainly suggests that there was a need in Europe for a dialogue between higher education research aiming to be relevant to practice and practitioners wanting to be aware of the available systematic knowledge on higher education and wanting to integrate this knowledge into their daily professional work. However, as will be discussed below, the research basis of EAIR remained clearly different from that of AIR even today.

In the mid-1990s, the German higher education expert Edgar Frackmann wrote an article on the state of higher education research in Europe for a conference on the state of higher education research worldwide (Sadlak and Altbach 1997). Frackmann (1997) observed three 'functional types' of higher education research in Europe:

- the national and system-wide support,
- institutional research and institutional management support,
- support on higher education as self-reflection.

This typology suggests that a similar 'map' of higher education research has emerged in Europe over the years as it already had existed in the U.S., even though higher education research in Europe has not yet reached the level of institutional stability as it had reached in the U.S. already some time ago. I do not share Frackmann's view completely. I perceived higher education research in Europe as less clearly demarcated in three areas than higher education research in the United States.

ACADEMIC RESEARCH ON HIGHER EDUCATION IN EUROPE

Academic higher education research in Europe is not delineated by academic positions for higher education programmes. Rather, first efforts of establishing higher education masters or doctor programmes only began to emerge in the late 1990s and these are still very small in number. In some European countries, educational departments showed some interest in higher education research, although higher education played a small role in teaching. In other European countries, academics of education departments hardly showed any interest in higher education at all.

Rather, we note that individual researchers from a broad range of disciplines were pioneers of higher education research in Europe. In addition, major policy concerns and priorities were behind the establishment of specific research units of higher education in the academic domain (cf. Teichler 1996).

In the 1960s, certainly the OECD was a major breeding ground for economists who became active in higher education research. The establishment of the Institute for Research in the Economics of Education (IREDU) of the Bourgogne University in Dijon (France), founded in the early 1970s, is an outgrowth of the popularity of the economics of education in the 1960s. The Institute covers all fields of education, but certainly contributed significantly to research on higher education.

Around 1970, various centres for teaching and learning were established at universities in Europe. These units combined research and service functions. Their staffs were not only recruited from education, psychology and sociology, but from a broad range of other fields as well. In some countries, the number and the size of these units declined rapidly after a short period of blossoming.

When debates spread about graduate employment and curricular relevance, the Centre for Research on Higher Education and Work was established at the University of Kassel (Germany) in the late 1970s; it is a interdisciplinary research unit whereby sociological concepts play a substantial role. When increasing attention was paid to issues of steering and management in higher education, the Centre for Higher Education Policy Studies was established in the mid-1980s at the Twente University in Enschede (The Netherlands); it was an interdisciplinary research unit at the beginning, and later became part of the faculty of public administration.

Two other examples of continuous research based on a sizeable number of scholars should be named. The Norwegian Institute of Research and Education in Oslo (Norway), which is known for its research on science and on the relationships between higher education and employment, certainly draws strongly from sociology and economics, but comprises other disciplines as well. A stronger single disciplinary focus is signalled in the name of the largest Finnish research group on higher education, the Research Unit for the Sociology of Education at the Turku University (Finland).

All these institutions for research on higher education which turned out to be successful and stable for a long period, had in common

- an emphasis on the academic basis of their research along with a readiness to undertake also research of a more applied nature sponsored by actors of policy and practice;
- a strong weight of one or two core thematic areas of research alongside a spread of research into other thematic areas;
- a core recruitment of staff from one or two disciplines along the readiness to integrate researchers from other disciplines.

Finally, there are many individual scholars active in higher education research for most of their academic life or for some period, who are based in various university faculties in the humanities and social sciences. Some of them are part of the 'invisible college' of higher education researchers in Europe while others consider themselves primarily as members of a disciplinary academic community.

The Consortium of Higher Education Researchers (CHER) which was founded in 1988, became the major institutional basis for the communication of academically-based researchers in Europe. CHER, which comprises also researchers from other parts in the world, conducts annual conferences with about 50 to 100 persons as internal communication among scholars.

POLICY AND PRACTICE-BASED RESEARCH

There is no publication available about the state of policy or practice-based research on higher education in Europe. In various countries, state institutes exist which address higher education either as the key area or as one of their domains (e.g. in the framework of education research or labour market research). A few universities have established small units for institutional research. In some countries, researchers whose institutional basis is linked to government, other supra-institutional agencies, or individual institutions of higher education have found ways of forming national networks, but as a rule, these researchers are hardly interrelated nationally.

There is not any network nationally or Europe-wide of policy and practice-based research of a similar strength and coverage as the AIR, the network of practice-based researchers in the United States. This holds true even though the number of persons active in higher education research who do not hold an academic position might be higher in Europe than the number of persons involved in higher education who hold academic positions.

FORA OF HIGHER EDUCATION EXPERTS

Instead, we note in Europe quite successful activities of various organisations which aim to stimulate the generation, presentation and dissemination of systematic knowledge on higher education without drawing clear borderlines between researchers, administrators involved in various types of research or information gathering activities, practitioners who understand themselves as experts of higher education as well as actors in higher education who are interested 'consumers' of higher education research or other sources of expert knowledge on higher education. We might call them higher education expert fora.

There are various structures of these fora. The EAIR is an association of individuals aiming to stimulate the communication among the various kinds of experts. The Institutional Management of Higher Education (IMHE) association under the umbrella of the OECD is a similar body of higher education institutions as members. Also most conferences held by the European Association of Universities (EAU), the association of the university rectors, and by many other associations are similar in this respect. Also, many meetings under the auspices of the UNESCO, the OECD and the Council of Europe have a similar character. The meetings have a hidden rule of conduct according to which the diverse actors who present their knowledge and views first of all present themselves similarly as experts on higher education and in this way act in similar roles. The distinct roles and modes of expertise ought to be presented only as secondary identities – at least in the course of these meetings.

The multitude of these experts' fora are a mixed blessing for higher education research. We note at least two dangers.

- The fora are tempting for researchers to undertake research and present research findings in a less ambitious and rigorous way than they consider acceptable among research peers. Thus, the quality of higher education research might be compromised.

- They encourage choices of themes in research which are welcome in those fora. These fora are likely to put a strong emphasis on the immediate areas of interest of the powerful actors in the higher education system: Issues of policy, system, governance, management and quality control are in the forefront, whereas curriculum development, guidance and counselling, teaching and learning processes on life and study of students play a marginal role. Thus, we note in higher education research in Europe a policy and management 'drift' and somewhat of a neglect of research on phenomena close to the key function of higher education, i.e. research, teaching and learning.

But, there are obvious opportunities as well.

- The fora provide the higher education researchers with an easily accessible platform to the nearest 'neighbours', i.e. the various types of experts partially involved in research or similar activities of information-gathering and the policy-makers and practitioners most interested in higher education research.

- The somewhat less rigorous border-line for presentations serve as encouragement for young higher education researchers to start their first major presentation in these fora rather than in academic conferences.

- In reverse, these fora certainly encourage professionals in administrative and policy functions to strengthen their involvement in research and thus certainly strengthen applied policy research and institutional research.

There are several Europe-based higher education journals published by associations and agencies often arranging these expert fora. For example, EAIR publishes "Tertiary Education and Management", IMHE and OECD "Journal of Higher Education Management and Policy", CEPES/UNESCO "Higher Education in Europe" and the International Association of Universities (IAU) "Higher Education Policy". The majority of these journals publish predominantly research articles, but, in contrast to typical research journals such as "Higher Education", they do not exclude other articles and they avoid any clear demarcation between research articles or other articles. The journal policies resemble the fora policies in principle, but they put a relatively stronger emphasis on the dissemination of research and the encouragement of actors of the higher education system to move their activities toward higher education research.

FUTURE OPTIONS FOR EAIR

EAIR never became, as its 'mother' body, the AIR in the United States, an association primarily for professional enhancement and communication among 'institutional researchers' in higher education. EAIR would have ceased to exist, if it tried to do so, because sufficient quantity of institutional researchers in Europe has not existed in the past. Instead, EAIR became the body in Europe exclusively serving a forum function for various types of higher education experts. Other agencies also play a role in stimulating and arranging similar fora, but EAIR is the only visible body in Europe exclusively focussing on this function. Heads of administration of individual higher education institutions as well as higher education researchers of various backgrounds played the strongest role in setting up annual EAIR fora which had to be more stimulating than those of other bodies involved in similar activities, because the fate of the EAIR depended exclusively on the success of these annual fora, a few additional workshops and the dissemination of the best presentations in a journal. Actually, around 400 participate in the annual EAIR forum, more than 100 present a paper, and about 20 of these papers are eventually published in the Tertiary Education and Management. Key themes addressed are policy, government and management as well as quality issues, but there is ample room for other themes as well.

There are reasons, though, to assume that EAIR cannot merely continue to operate in the same format. The context is changing. We note a growth of bodies which organise similar fora as part of their activities. We observe an increase of higher educational professionals, i.e. academically trained professionals of higher education, who are neither primarily researchers and teachers nor part of the core administration, but rather have service or specialised administrative function, i.e. knowledge transfer, guidance, programme development, international relations, etc.; they clearly are professionals having a strong interest in systematic knowledge on higher education. And we can perceive a growth of knowledge production in higher education which would not be termed 'higher education research', e.g. statistics and evaluation.

The EAIR as the most visible exclusive body for arranging expert fora on higher education in Europe serves its niche best by strengthening the role of higher education research in these fora and by encouraging stronger research activities among those persons whose role is not primarily defined by higher education research but who are interested in playing a role in higher education research. There could be various ways to strengthen the research function.

Higher education research is sometimes criticised as focussing to strongly on the 'down-to-earth' issues of the daily life of higher education (see for example Scott 2000). Fora could stimulate a view on more salient secular issues of higher education and thus provide a new framework for the analysis of the daily life of higher education (cf. also Teichler 2003).

Higher education research is also criticised as neglecting the real information needs of the policy makers and practitioners. In general, there is little information available regarding the ways the 'consumers' of systematic knowledge on higher education are actually 'consuming' (see Kogan and Henkel 2000). EAIR could choose the knowledge needs of the policy-makers and practitioners as an area of investigation.

Finally, EAIR could move some steps in the direction of its mother organisation, i.e. the AIR in the United States. It could help to provide a professional identity for higher education professionals partly involved in research on higher education and could encourage their activities in favour of establishing institutional research at institutions of higher education in Europe. No matter whether institutional research will increase in separate units or as part of the work role of higher educational professionals, their research activities are likely to be enhanced if EAIR becomes a strong 'home' for these activities rather than just serves them as one of the many types of higher education 'experts'.

REFERENCES

Becher, R. I. (1992). Introduction: Disciplinary perspectives on higher education. In: Clark, B.R. & Neave, G.R. (eds.), The Encyclopedia of Higher Education (pp. 1763–1776). Oxford: Pergamon Press.

El-Khawas, E. (2000). Research, Policy and Practice: Assessing their actual and potential linkages. In: Teichler, U. and Sadlak, J. (eds.), Higher Education and Research: Its Relationship to Policy and Practice (pp. 37–46). Oxford: Pergamon/IAU Press.

Frackmann, E. (1997). Research on higher education in Western Europe: From policy advice to self-reflection. In: Sadlak, J. and Altbach, P.G. (eds.), Higher Education Research at the Turn of the New Century (pp. 107-136). Paris: UNESCO Press; New York and London: Garland Publ.

Gibbons, M., Limoges, C., Nowotny, H., Schwartzman, S., Scott, P. & Trow, M. (1995). The New Production of Knowledge. London: Sage.

Kogan, M. & Henkel, M. (2000). Future dimensions of higher education policy research. In: Schwarz, S. and Teicher, U. (eds.), The Institutional Basis of Higher Education Research (pp. 25-43). Dordrecht: Kluwer Academic Publishers.

Sadlak, J. & Altbach, P.G. (1997). Higher Education Research at the Turn of the New Century. Paris: UNESCO Press; New York and London: Garland Publ.

Schwarz, S. & Teichler, U. (eds.). The Institutional Basis of Higher Education Research. Dordrecht: Kluwer Academic Publishers.

Scott, P. (2000). Higher education research in the light of a dialogue between policy-makers and practitioners. In: Teichler, U. and Sadlak, J., Higher Education Research: Its Relationship to Policy and Practice (pp. 123-147). Oxford: Pergamon/IAU Press.

Teichler, U. (1996). Comparative Higher Education: Potentials and Limits. Higher Education, 32(4), 431–465.

Teichler, U. The future of higher education and the future of higher education research. Tertiary Education and Management. (Forthcoming.)

Teichler, U. & Sadlak, J. (eds.) (2000). Higher Education Research: Its Relationship to Policy and Practice. Oxford: Pergamon/IAU Press.

MICHAEL SHATTOCK

RESEARCH, ADMINISTRATION AND UNIVERSITY MANAGEMENT: WHAT CAN RESEARCH CONTRIBUTE TO POLICY?

Abstract. This paper shows how in four important case studies research into management issues directly and profoundly influenced the development of a major university. It argues that research is an essential component of policy formation for universities and that opportunities, such as are provided by the EAIR Forum for university managers, whether they are academics or administrators, to think, research and write about university issues, make a critical contribution to institutional effectiveness.

INTRODUCTION

The first EAIR Conference I attended was at Trier in 1989 and I gave a paper analysing the common characteristics of three UK universities which had been subjected to external scrutiny by the UK funding authority, then still the University Grants Committee (UGC), because of their inability to anticipate sharp downturns in their budgets. The paper, which I recall attracted mostly UK attendees at the Conference because very few participants from other countries could imagine their institutions facing this kind of situation, argued that a common feature of the three universities was an absorption in the internal logic of their own positions and an absolute failure to pay attention to the external environment. One of the three reports said that the university concerned:

> was an administered rather than a strategically managed institution; it had a large and conservative Senatus, committed to the rights of the individual faculty member to control his own affairs; it felt it had special obligations in respect of the professional and cultural needs of a unique region of Scotland and indeed, in some subjects, of Scotland as a whole, and it felt that central government had the responsibility to ensure that it (the university) had the financial and other resources necessary to fulfill its academic and regional roles. (Segal Quince Wicksteed 1988).

My paper tried to look at the organisational and other factors which contributed to these inward looking cultures, and the extent to which the external pressure exercised by the reports that had been written for the UGC (one by myself) had been successful in provoking change. Writing the paper was useful for me because it served to emphasise some important general considerations which, in the rescue of University College, Cardiff, in which I had been deeply involved, I had tended to invest with only local significance, and it reinforced my perception that an important role of any senior university manager must be to understand the context in which his or her institution had to operate and what were the environmental trends that might affect that institution's future. It was not enough, in other words, to try to manage the internal activities of an institution; you had to look outwards to the political, economic and social trends that were apparent in society at large; in particular you had to try to 'read'

R. Begg (ed.), The Dialogue between Higher Education Research and Practice, 55–66.
© 2003 *Kluwer Academic Publishers. Printed in the Netherlands.*

the funding bureaucracies to get a sense of what pressures they were under and the directions in which they were being pushed. Such conclusions anticipated, in a university context, the findings of writers about business such as Pettigrew and Whipp (1993), Garvin (1993), Valberda (1998) and Ghoshal and Bartlett (1999), all of whom emphasise the importance of adapting institutional strategies to environmental circumstances.

I do not know what benefit the audience got from the paper but I derived a good deal from writing it, both practically and when, more than a decade later, I gave a plenary lecture at the EAIR Conference at Lund in 1999 entitled 'Strategic management in universities in an age of increasing institutional self reliance', later published in Tertiary Education and European Management (2002), where what I said about the environmental context drew unconsciously from that earlier paper as well as from Barbara Sporn's Adaptive University Structures (1999) and I am grateful to EAIR for encouraging me to undertake the research and give the paper. It has always seemed to me that one of the most important functions of the annual Forum is to encourage university administrators/managers to distil their experience in papers and to broaden it by comparative and other research. Administrators/managers are not natural researchers, partly because they lack the time and partly because they tend to live in the present dealing with business that has to be dispatched expeditiously and find it difficult to make the space to reflect on institutional management problems from a research, or perhaps more realistically, from an evidence-based, perspective.

In Europe, in spite of the words 'Institutional Research' being included in EAIR's title, we have not formalised institutional research in the way that has happened in the US. There are, I believe, two reasons for this. The first is that the academic community, which in the past played a dominant role in the running of universities, was not interested in investing resources into solving managerial problems. Lord Ashby, a distinguished botanist and enlightened vice-chancellor wrote in 1963:

> Academic decisions are on the whole made by academic men...... yet all over the country these groups of scholars, who would not take a decision about the shape of a leaf or the derivation of a work or the author of a manuscript without painstakingly assembling the evidence, make decisions about admissions policy, size of universities, staff-student ratios, content of courses and similar issues based on dubious assumptions, scrappy data and mere hunch. (Ashby 1963).

What he said entirely echoed my own experience working in a large (for then) civic university in the early 1960s, when for example I produced, on my own initiative (and because I shared an office with a persuadable university data processing officer) a paper which showed for the first time where we drew our students from, how many were from a local, how many from a national catchment and described a number of other significant characteristics of the student body. The senate greeted the effort with curiosity and interest but never considered that it might have implications for policy. A second reason is that universities, as Segal Quince Wicksteed were to say two decades later, were administered not managed, and sought to appoint administrative staff whose role was much more to implement decisions taken by academic committees and much less to propose policies or take managerial decisions that affected the running of the institution. There was no incentive for administrators to research institutional problems and come up with strategic solutions precisely because they were administrators rather than managers. The move from élite to mass higher education, the consequent acute pressure on resources, the search for value for money, and the intensified interventions by the state have changed that but there remains a disinclination, even now, to invest resources into assembling data, undertaking analysis and doing detailed research into issues of strategic importance for higher education institutions. We still like to take decisions on the hoof rather than subject them to the kind of research scrutiny that we would apply in our own academic disciplines.

It is not possible to write a general account of how institutional research has changed the way institutions are managed because, although the climate has changed markedly, the level of investment in institutional research remains perilously low. What therefore I propose to do in this chapter is to draw on my own experience of four instances which show how research can impact on the strategic direction that institutions may take in the hope that it will offer encouragement to others and arguments that will persuade institutions to invest accordingly.

THE ADMISSIONS PROCESS

In the UK, all applications for undergraduate entry to higher education have to be made through the Universities and Colleges Applications System (UCAS), each applicant being able to make five choices. This provides a wealth of data which can be used strategically by institutions as to where they stand in terms of the strength of their application field and the level of their offer course by course against competitor institutions. During the early 1970s, the University of Warwick attracted a great deal of unfavourable publicity because of a continuing incidence of student activism, and applications for places fell sharply. At the same time the University was anxious to expand to what would have been then a medium sized institution of about 5000 students. Many of its competitors were able to expand more quickly because they had strong application fields and, since resources followed student numbers, were able to found new departments and strengthen older ones. Warwick was in difficulty because it was not attracting enough applicants to justify growth, the applicants were not well qualified compared to the intake to comparable universities and the student failure and dropout rates, had climbed alarmingly.

The situation was so serious that the University was persuaded to fund a three year research post to work with me in identifying what steps we should take. One characteristic of our admissions was the number of mature (over 21) candidates the University accepted and concern was expressed that this represented a lowering of quality (that is, we were accepting mature students because we were receiving insufficient applications from well educated and well qualified 18 year olds). Our first enquiry therefore was in relation to the performance of our mature intakes. The results were reported to the senate and published in Research in Education: the evidence showed that over the period 1965 (when the University took its first students) to 1971 mature students were concentrated in the Politics, Philosophy and Sociology Departments (which also happened to be where the most radical students were), and that they graduated with better degrees than non-mature students. Moreover, where mature students had not taken 'A' level examinations and were admitted under a special procedure of providing examples of written work these students obtained significantly better degrees than students of all ages entering with conventional qualifications (Walker 1975). This effectively ended the argument as to whether accepting mature students was weakening the intake academically, and bears heavily on the argument, much invoked in the UK in 2003 by some universities that mature students may be expected to have higher dropout rates than 18 year olds. Of course, in the period 1965-71, mature students received maintenance grants and the personal financial pressures were consequently much less but we did a similar study in 1998 of students we were admitting through Access or 2+2 programmes, where the first two years were given in FE colleges, and interestingly we came up with a comparable result.

The research in 1975 went on to look at what influenced applications to particular institutions. The conventional wisdom at that time was that the dominant influence was head teachers or careers masters but our research showed very clearly that sixth formers made their decisions much more individually on the basis (in that order) of the university's prospectus, information from friends and acquaintances and advice from their actual teachers and that two factors in particular affected whether they accepted an offer of a place at Warwick: one was the actual syllabus of the course and the second was their impression of the University when they visited it. (Shattock & Walker 1977). This had an immediate impact on the University's approach to the admissions process: expenditure on the prospectus, and the numbers of copies printed was doubled, the encouragement of teachers conferences at the University was quietly dropped, and maximum effort was made to encourage sixth formers themselves to visit the University. (Because the University was new, and had an out of town campus a visit was much more likely to confirm a student's choice than might have been the case at a university like Leeds located in a well known provincial city). An equally influential piece of research was an exercise to write to all candidates who refused a Warwick offer of a place which produced the remarkable, and humbling reply from 80% of the respondents that a major factor was the University's slowness in processing the applications and communicating an offer. This prompted a major review of the admissions office and of the speed of decision-making by departmental selectors.

One last piece of research was done jointly with colleagues at the local polytechnic and the college of education to see whether there were differences in the factors prompting students to apply to institutions within three miles of one another. The striking message to emerge was not the differences but the similarities, particularly between the polytechnic and the university. University applicants were better qualified and much less likely to be locally based but all three sets of applicants put 'to obtain access to more interesting jobs', 'to widen personal outlook and experience' and 'to gain a knowledge of an academic subject for itself' in that order as their prime motives for entering higher education, rather than directly vocational, sporting or cultural reasons. They confirmed, once again, that the prospectus was by far the most effective factor affecting their choice of institution. (Walker, Cunnington, Richards & Shattock 1979)

Having much improved its understanding of what factors influenced institutional choice the University invested in a schools liaison office whose task was to ensure that the University maximised its impact on schools, and through them to their pupils. Recognition that visiting the University was important led to a wholesale and continuous review of how the campus looked, the establishment of open days, the training of student guides to show potential applicants round and the improvement of departmental presentations. And most important, we began to collect market research data of who attended open days and from what schools and colleges, how many of them subsequently applied, were made offers of places and actually accepted them at Warwick, together with feedback on the visits etc. Over 15 years the University tripled its number of applications, now 10 for every place, pushed itself up to be the sixth highest A level scoring entry in the UK and turned its open days into major events with

4,000 applicants and their parents attending. One downside of this success was the fall off in the proportion of mature students being accepted via this entry route and the University has had to open an alternative entry through 2+2 degrees via local colleges of further education and part time degrees to maintain its mature entry strand. Another, was that as the position improved the methods of data collection, analysis and consequential changes in practice became market sensitive and not publishable. Perhaps it was a sign of the times that our first director of schools liaison resigned to write novels but our second was head hunted to be director of a well known marketing company which had a large higher education portfolio.

STRATEGIC DECISION-MAKING

By the late 1970s various new trends in UK higher education were beginning to become apparent: funding was getting tighter, competition between universities was becoming more explicit and doubts were being expressed about whether, under Mrs. Thatcher, all universities could be expected to survive. Warwick had ridden the storm of student dissent in the early 1970s, its student numbers had grown and it had taken over the next door college of education which had brought a new activity, teacher training, into the subject mix and had increased its stock of buildings. In particular, a collection of academic departments or initiatives begun in the mid 1970s – classics, film studies, environmental studies, theatre studies and psychology were beginning to diversify the academic programme and were making claims for resources which competed internally with the well established departments which were seeking to strengthen their staffing to compete more vigorously with other universities. The University decided that it had to take a longer look at its future and set up an ad hoc group to produce a report. In fact the results of the group's discussions were not very remarkable except that it accepted a recommendation that the University needed to invest much more time and energy in establishing better academic and other data to improve decision-making and senate authorised a new process of data collection which was first brought together in 1980, and given the de-politicised title, the Academic Data Base (now called simply Academic Statistics).

This may seem to be a routine and unremarkable decision but it was not. One of Warwick's strengths was its internal resource allocation machinery under which the council (the governing body) devolved resources for academic development to the senate for a senate committee to allocate between academic departments and services as it saw fit. Over the 1970s this committee (the estimates and grants committee) had combined the use of academic judgement with the evaluation of a quantitative data about student load and staff-student ratios to allocate resources for new academic posts, support posts and consumables on the basis of a combination of departmental submissions, face to face cross examination of departmental chairs and the overall strategic priorities agreed at senate and council. Since the resources available were finite and never sufficient to match the requirements of ambitious departments the process was competitive between departments and fraught with difficulty in, for example, deciding between the claims for a new professorship in History against a lecturer post in Chemistry.

What the Academic Database sought to provide with time series stretching back five years was the data which would assist such decisions. But right at the beginning it was agreed first that the data must be made widely available for discussion both in academic departments and in faculty boards, as well as at planning committees, senate and council, and, second that it must be published early in the academic year in November (that is by the November senate meeting) so that data trends up to and including the previous year could influence decisions in the current year. Achieving this early publication meant that each office in the Registry had to contribute its own data under the editorship of the Academic Registrar, rather than a separate unit being set up. We were anxious to disclaim that the Database contained performance indicators (the wording of the disclaimer is almost identical in 2002 with that of 1980) but in practice comparing data year on year and by comparing performance between departments particularly in research across the UK the statistics constituted, if not performance indicators, a powerful incentive to improve performance. Over the years the report has been improved and new lines of comparative data have been introduced but it has remained the bedrock of academic planning, resource allocation and measuring quality in the University, and the source for impassioned debates about the direction of the University, what to do about departments that are falling behind and how the University should invest in success.

The current edition divides itself into undergraduate statistics, postgraduate statistics, student careers and first destination statistics, research grant and contract data and includes data on scores from the Research Assessment Exercise (RAE) and Teaching Assessment ratings. At the undergraduate level you can see the numbers of applications, their regional source, the entry levels, the national market share for each degree programme, the completion rates and degree classifications, with comparisons with other Russell and '94 Group Universities discipline by discipline, as well as analysis by social class, and ethnicity, and home country of overseas students. Similar data is held on postgraduate students except that the comparative data is not available in the absence of a UCAS for postgraduate applicants. Careers/first destination data is covered subject by subject for undergraduates and postgraduates. For research, the tables break down individual grants and contracts awarded and research income, and compares average research income per academic staff member by subject comparatively across the UK university system (University of Warwick 2002).

This is powerful data, the more powerful because continuous analysis has identified how it can be used comparatively to assess Warwick departments not just against one another but against competitor departments in other universities. The chair of department who argues for an increased staff member to match rising student demand or to capitalise on a rising research profile had better research his/her case carefully because the committee who he or she addresses will have the same data before them. Such data is critical to making good strategic academic decisions whether at the micro level of granting a new post or at the more macro level of closing a department or investing in it. Most important the data is timely and is debated widely so that the University is constantly aware of its competitive position and the trends that have placed it there. In a market driven and competitive university system this kind of statistical data is crucial, not because an institution should be ruled by data but because such decisions, as Ashby above suggests, should be informed by data, especially data produced routinely rather than data assembled quickly to rationalise decisions taken intuitively or on other grounds. If Warwick has been academically successful in the last two decades it is partly because it has armed itself more professionally than most of its competitors with the data it needs to inform its strategy.

CHANGING THE ACADEMIC STRUCTURE: CREATING A GRADUATE SCHOOL

By the late 1980s, Warwick had weathered the financial turmoil of the 1981 cuts and had performed much better comparatively than expected in the first RAE in 1986. It had been identified as a leading research university, but its vice-chancellor and senior managers knew that it nevertheless had some important weaknesses. One of these was that its graduate population represented only about 25% of the student body and its PhD numbers compared unfavourably with universities also laying claim to be leading research universities. In 1989-90, Professor Bob Burgess (now Vice-Chancellor of the University of Leicester) and I persuaded the University to create a Graduate School along US university lines with the aim of shifting the balance of the student population more towards graduate numbers and encouraging a more centralised concern for postgraduate matters.

However, persuading our colleagues and the senate of the importance of the idea, and the fundamental shift in thinking and organisation which it entailed was one thing but bringing it about and making it work in practice was another. What were the fundamental organisational concepts that made US graduate schools so effective? How could a successful graduate school be grafted on to a university that prized the quality of its undergraduate programmes as highly as Warwick did? Operationally, what should be the balance of powers between a centralised graduate school and academic departments some of whom had already built up substantial doctoral schools?

An important element in resolving these and other issues was the University's sponsorship of a young administrator, Dr. John Hogan, now Registrar of the University of Newcastle, to take a Fullbright University Administrative Fellowship to spend three months in the Graduate School of the University of Wisconsin at Madison in 1991. His 60 page report Graduate Schools: The Organisation of Graduate Education in the USA (1991), represented a comprehensively researched account of the history of graduate education in the US, how it was organised both nationally and at the institutional level in research intensive universities, how recruitment was handled, and the interrelationship of graduate deans and departmental heads. It offered recommendations to Warwick and to the UK university system. It was indeed a remarkable document for a young Assistant Registrar to have written and provided the blueprint not only for the detailed organisation of the Graduate School at Warwick but also for the creation of a UK-wide Council of UK Graduate Schools, based on the US Council of Graduate Schools, of which Burgess became the first chair and Hogan himself the first secretary.

Warwick's reorganisation of graduate education into a Graduate School, with Hogan its first secretary, had the immediate effect of prioritising the needs of postgraduates for scholarships, residential accommodation, library resources, and representation which sharply re-balanced the University away from an implicit concentration on undergraduate matters. In parallel with the University's action the graduate students themselves set up a Postgraduate Council within the Students Union which represented graduate's social and other interests within the campus. From 25% of the student population the proportion rose to over 40% comprising about 7000 students in 2002-03 (about five times the population in 1991-02) with some masters programmes attracting application fields as large as popular first degrees. For a matter of three months salary and some inconvenience in covering John Hogan's duties while he was away in the US the University acquired the organisational confidence to proceed with its plan and Hogan's report was the inspiration for the creation of a national body for graduate education.

RESISTING FASHION: MODULARISATION AND SEMESTERISATION

One of the most remarkable features of the creation of the Council of UK Graduate Schools was the extent to which universities copied the Warwick graduate school initiative as if it was a kind of organisational elixir which would transform institutional performance and without apparent thought as to whether the initiative was appropriate in their own circumstances. It was noticeable, however, that some of the strongest universities in graduate education, such as Oxbridge and Imperial College, did not join the rush. The organisational framework worked well at Warwick because it had been researched and because it cohered with the institution's strategy and became integral to it; it was not an add on or stimulated by fashion. At almost exactly the same time another academic bandwagon (as the graduate school idea was to become) was rolling through UK higher education – proposals for modularisation and semesterisation. In a formal sense these proposals first surfaced at a conference for interested universities held at the University of Kent in October 1990, but they had been discussed for some time and were regarded as potentially timely because of the sudden rise in the UK age participation rate. This acceleration in growth confirmed the UK's transition from elite to mass higher education and raised questions as to whether the time was not ripe to overhaul the traditional (elite?) single honours degree structure and adopt the US model of modular degrees, said to offer a welcome flexibility to the new student clientele, who were thought to be less interested in concentrating their study in a single discipline. A modular programme demanded a two semester, rather than a three term academic year, and, since the second semester might end earlier than the traditional three term year, another benefit was that a third semester could be added in the summer to pick up a further part of the new clientele who it was thought would be studying for credits in the summer semester to build a credit based degree over a period of years. This would also, it was argued, give better use of university plant.

These ideas were brought to a head at the Kent conference. Warwick had sent an academic representative who returned saying, in effect, that he had seen the future and it worked! Warwick had always had an extremely flexible academic structure with students following core disciplinary degree programmes, or joint degrees, but with opportunities to take options in other departments: mathematicians, for example, were famous for taking film studies courses in their final year, and many students chose to do a business studies option at some point in their three years. The Kent convert's enthusiasm prompted some concern, but rather than reject it the senate was persuaded to create a short term research post reporting to the Registrar to investigate the academic evidence and arguments for modularisation and semesterisation, and we were fortunate to be able to appoint an Oxford trained former Education Officer for Birmingham, Stan Green, who was set the task of reading the academic literature about modular degrees and preparing a report which tested the evidence for the claims that were being made. In the meantime the support for modularisation nationally grew. A second conference at the University of Bradford in April 1991, heard arguments from the vice-chancellor there based on his previous experience at the City Polytechnic, Hong Kong that the benefits of modularisation were:

- more flexible course design
- better use of staff time
- more student choice
- easier for credit accumulation
- equality for full time and part time study
- objectives, learning strategies and assessment methods had been re-thought

In June 1991 the Committee of Vice-Chancellors and Principals (CVCP) issued a paper entitled 'Modular Curriculum and Structure' (1991) which identified 'rapid and growing interest among universities' in modularisation and argued that 'a consensus model' needed to be developed. The paper claimed the following reasons for embarking on such an extensive overhaul of undergraduate teaching:

- it encouraged a review of educational objectives learning strategies and assessment methods
- it improved the quality/economy of teaching/learning flexibility to accommodate an increasing diversity of entrant
- it accommodated off campus student placement
- it enabled part time study
- it increased the number of pathways through the total provision of an institution
- it facilitated transfer between institutions
- it identified new inter disciplinary pathways
- it spread the examination load (because students would be examined at the end of each semester)

The paper argued that 'The benefits to a university are considerable' and reported that the CVCP Academic Advisory Committee was formally recommending universities to adopt a two semester structure.

In September 1991 a second Kent conference was held, attended by 40 pre-1992 universities and its report prepared by the Standing Conference for University Entrance (SCUE) concluded that: 'it is clear that higher education is moving steadily towards the flexible provision that a modular structure can offer' (1991). Such a move was warmly endorsed by the Secretary of State and the Funding Council created a special fund to encourage universities to undertake the necessary changes.

In the meantime, the Warwick project to investigate the benefits of modularity and semesterisation was proceeding and in October 1991 Green produced his first report. After intensive reading and consultation he concluded that:

> There are no established norms or comparative research findings to take this beyond the level of subjective judgement..... The absence of basic research nationally is a deficiency and .....nothing of value is available for reliable use at this stage.

He suggested that the academic advantages claimed for modularity in terms of flexibility and breaking away from traditional subject boundaries 'need to be treated with caution' and that Warwick already offered 'real diversity across the range of degrees. In answer to claims that modular programmes were more economical, he wrote:

> I have not been able to find any significant research into the effectiveness of modular structures.....in terms of their objectives and in comparison with other structural forms, or

in terms of relative costs. Indeed there does not seem to be any statistical base nationally
from which operational research might start. (Green 1991a).

A month later he reported to the Registrar that a recent inspectorate report on a
polytechnic that had developed modular structures over many years had confirmed that
the scheme produced no cost benefits and where economies of scale in the shared
provision and common teaching could be identified they were more than balanced by
the increased costs of administration and examination. Moreover modularity produced
no alleviation of the pressure on the academic timetable and the use of teaching rooms.

Green's second report (1991b) was by no means entirely negative and included a
detailed working out with examples of how the Warwick academic programme could be
modularised and how the three term structure could be semesterised. The report was
widely debated within the University. But the academic counter-arguments to
modularisation were considerable: a two semester programme would cut into research
time; breaking courses into 'bite size' modules, and examining mid year would devalue
the academic benefit of year long courses, particularly in humanities and social studies;
and a statistical assessment commissioned by the senate's academic policy committee of
the extent to which students took courses outside their departments showed that there
was no advantage to be gained at Warwick from one of the prime claims advanced for
modular courses that they encouraged greater interdisciplinarity; a two semester
programme would severely curtail the University's ability to generate income from the
external use of its facilities, especially for conferences, which was an important element
in its residential building programme. On the other hand, the discussion lead to
questions being raised about the lack of regulation in examination weightings for
optional courses and the lack of a common 'tariff' in the Warwick academic offerings.
This prompted the need for a review and the overhaul of these arrangements and the
establishment of a clearly laid down credit points system, which has subsequently
benefited the introduction of new programmes.

Warwick decisively rejected modularisation and semesterisation at a time when all
over the country universities were adopting it largely because so many vice-chancellors
and senior bodies were encouraging them to do so. Now more than a decade later it is
often quoted as the real beginning of managerialism and many universities pre-and
post-1992 are trying to put back the clock. Mid year examinations have greatly added
to the burden on individual academics especially as student numbers have grown and
the requirements of quality assessment procedures have intensified. The number of
students choosing to transfer institutions and to take advantage of the Credit
Accumulation and Transfer System (CATS) has proved to be minimal. Third semester
arrangements have failed to attract students. From the research perspective, it may be
significant that none of the universities at the top of the RAE research league tables
have adopted modular structures or have changed from a three term year to two
semesters.

It is now clear that modularisation and semesterisation, whatever the benefits for
some institutions, represented in Birnbaum's terms, a classic 'management fad'
(Birnbaum 2000) which universities adopted, against the many criticisms lower down in
the academic community, because it was thought to be an intrinsic part of a new
academic order: it was unresearched and introduced as an act of faith. In the mid
1990s, Warwick thought it might be isolated by its decision not to join the party but
now it regards it as an integral strategic contribution to its success and academic well
being over the last decade and it is much envied in some quarters by those who made

the change. That decision, however, was a direct result of commissioning research and weighing up the evidence, before rushing headlong to judgement.

CONCLUSION

This paper has selected for separate examination four areas in one University where research, or in the case of the Academic Database well researched data, has been deployed either to improve the management of the University, or in the latter case to enable it to avoid being bounced by fashion into a reform which would have been detrimental to its academic interests. In all four cases, the University was strengthened by following the research findings and in none of them did the University hire external consultants although in two it appointed researchers on short-term contracts. The research has produced long term benefits: the research on the admissions process laid down a marker for the analysis of data and operational efficiency which is very clearly still strongly observed and the scrutiny of recruitment performance is a matter of interest across the University; the impact of the annual production of time series of data on issues relevant to resource allocation leads every year to debate in senate and council as to the University's comparative position in UK league tables; the internal change of structure to create a central Graduate School based on Hogan's research on models in the US remain an important safeguard of the University's commitment to graduate teaching; finally the research into modularisation and semesterisation prevented the University from being drawn into a radical reform of academic process driven for the most part by institutional 'me too ism' rather than by any evidence of proven benefit.

It is not the purpose of this paper to suggest that research into higher education management issues was lacking in other institutions, or that evidence-based management did not exist elsewhere but to identify some, amongst a number of examples, at one university which individually and collectively had a profound effect on the way it developed. The moral is that universities need to think harder about their management problems than they often do, or feel they have time to do. Strategic decisions are too often made on hunch or prejudice, or even for sectional advantage, rather than after a clear sighted review or on the basis of thorough investigation. Institutional management is not a science but it is still too often seen as a part time activity in which professionals have only a limited voice. This paper is intended to demonstrate that successful university management requires as great a willingness to research issues before taking decisions or to base policies on researched evidence as company management might be expected to demonstrate before embarking on large investments. University managers, whether academics or administrators need a forum such as EAIR provides to stimulate them to think, research and write about university issues because this is essential to the effectiveness of their contribution to their institutions.

REFERENCES

Ashby, E. (1963). Decision-making in the academic world. *Sociological Review*, Keele.
Birnbaum, R. (2000). Management Fads in Higher Education. Jossey Bass: San Francisco.
CVCP (1991). Modular Curriculum and Structure. 6 June.
Garvin, D.A. (1993). Building a learning organisation, *Harvard Business Review*, Vol. 71(4).
Ghoshal, S. & Bartlett, C. (1999). The Individualised Corporation. Heinman: London.

Green, S. (1991a). An Investigation into the Adaptation of Warwick Degree Programmes to a Modular Structure. University of Warwick.

Green, S. (1991b). An Examination of the Adaptation of Warwick Degree Programmes to a Modular Structure. University of Warwick.

Hogan, J. (1991). Graduate Schools: The Organisation of Graduate Education in the USA. University of Warwick.

Pettigrew, A.M. & Whipp, R. (1991). Managing Change for Competitive Success. Blackwell: Oxford.

SCUE (1991). Modularity. Standing Conference on University Entrance, 7 October.

Segal Quince Wicksteed (1988). Review of the Financial Situation and Prospects of the University of Aberdeen. A report to the University Grants Committee.

Shattock, M.L. and Walker, P.A. (1977). The factors influencing student choice of university: a report of an investigation at Warwick. *Research in Education*, 18.

Shattock, M.L. (2000). Strategic management in European universities in an age of increasing institutional self reliance. *Tertiary Education and Management*, 6(2).

Sporn, B. (1999). Adaptive University Structures. Jessica Kingsley: London.

University of Warwick (2002). Academic Statistics. University of Warwick.

Walker, P.A. (1975). University performance of mature students. *Research in Education*, 14.

Walker, P.A., Cunnington, J.L., Richards, M.A. & Shattock, M.L. (1979). Factors influencing entry at a university, a polytechnic and a college of education. *Higher Education Review*, 11(3).

PART 3

CURRENT STATE OF KNOWLEDGE AND THE FUTURE

LEE HARVEY AND BERIT ASKLING

QUALITY IN HIGHER EDUCATION

Abstract. From having been seen as an implicit element in university learning and teaching, and thus also a natural part of academics' responsibilities, the quality issue emerged in the 1990s as a topic of concern for politicians, institutional leaders, and a variety of other stakeholders. This concern emerged from a 'package' of simultaneous changes affecting higher education, such as the devolution of authority, new public sector management, restrictions on funding, expansion of student numbers and the like; these all were manifested in claims for external quality monitoring. The chapter gives an overview of different purposes of quality monitoring and also different forms of monitoring procedures. The question of the impact of external quality monitoring is also raised and discussed. The authors suggest that the catalytic function of monitoring for internal improvements within institutions ought to be emphasised.

INTRODUCTION

The 1990s has been the decade of quality in higher education. There had been mechanisms for ensuring the quality of higher education for decades prior to the 1990s, including the external examiner system in the UK and other Commonwealth countries, the American system of accreditation, and government ministerial control in much of Europe and elsewhere in the world. The 1990s, though, saw a change in the approach to higher education quality.

The change occurred for many reasons, in part pragmatic and in part ideological. Quality had by tradition been seen as an implicit and natural element of university-level learning and research and an integrated part of academics' professional responsibilities. This changed in the 1990s, with a requirement that higher education institutions should demonstrate, through their institutional leaders and expressed in comparable measures, the quality of its activities. Where institutions were used to see excellence or transformation as the self-evident key indicator of higher education quality, governments now emphasised value-for-money and fitness-for-purpose. In so doing, quality, as an implicit, self-evident property of higher education became transformed into a mechanism of control: an alien process of accountability and compliance that seemed to have no relation to the very essence of higher learning.

The initial introduction of governmental procedures for evaluating quality by focusing on indicators were, however, in the 1990s, gradually followed by the elaboration of more varied monitoring procedures. The governments' eagerness to get a grasp of what happens in the expanding higher education sector and to gain legitimacy for such measures, and at the same time, to encourage the institutions to respond to new challenges by improving their internal capacity for development and change, opened for variation in procedures and methods. The devolution of authority was emphasised and the contradictory elements of improvement and accountability in national arrangements for quality assurance were emphasised. References were made to the responsibilities of the institutions and their staff for monitoring and developing quality.

In this chapter, we shall give an overview of the quality issue, how it started and how it developed into a variety of monitoring procedures and, in addition, awoke a

69

R. Begg (ed.), The Dialogue between Higher Education Research and Practice, 69–83.

concern for the core missions of higher education, leadership and management, organisational development and, not the least, quality in teaching and student learning.

A POLITICAL CONCERN FOR QUALITY

As higher education expanded in many countries from the mid-1980s, encouraged by governmental concerns about the growth of knowledge-based economies and the role of higher education in being able to compete in a globalised world (DES 1985), their institutions came under the spotlight of new public sector management. More graduates were needed but there was no more public money to pay for them.

New public-sector management (Politt 1993; Bleiklie 1998), introduced at that time, was about improving the efficiency and effectiveness of the public services, in short, ensuring that necessary public services were produced at less cost to the government and hence the taxpayer. Higher education has not been immune from new management dogma. Indeed, there has been a notable retreat by governments from full support for higher education. In some countries, this has meant, for example, reducing student grants and introducing loans, introducing competition between institutions for students and research funds. The rubric of more for less, underpinning new public sector management, became the underpinning quality indicator for higher education in many countries.

Already in 1985, in the United Kingdom (UK), the government had expressed concern about quality in higher and the best way to ensure that there was accountability for the way that public money was spent. The Jarratt Report (CVCP 1985) on university efficiency recommended that the system as a whole should identify and fulfil clear objectives and achieve value for money. It proposed inter alia that performance indicators be developed to cover both inputs and outputs designed for intra- and inter-university comparison.

The Green paper (DES 1985) subsequently indicated the government's concern that higher education should contribute more effectively to the improvement of the performance of the economy. It suggested performance indicators such as 'the success of students in obtaining jobs, their relative salaries, and their reported performance in employment, and by reference to the international standing of our academic qualifications'. In addition, it paved the way for comparative judgements by external agencies. However, the Green Paper also stressed that the primary responsibility for preserving and enhancing quality rested with each institution, a principle from which nearly 20 years of quality initiatives in the UK has never wavered, whatever the practice. The Green Paper recommended that systems for monitoring and controlling quality should be explicit and open in the interests of accountability.

In the Netherlands, during the same period, there were significant changes in the structure and governance of higher education. The government's policy was explicit in Higher Education: Autonomy and Quality (Ministry for Education and Science 1985). The statement suggested that the existing administrative and legislative framework was no longer optimal to meet future demand. The central proposal was to increase the autonomy of the institutions by abolishing centralised regulations and introducing retrospective quality control. The intention was to allow the system to respond quickly and flexibly to market needs. In return for greater autonomy, institutions would be expected to develop their own systems of quality control and assurance that would demonstrate accountability for the use of public funds. (Goedegebuure et al. 1990).

France, one of the other early European pioneers of external quality monitoring introduced the Comité National d'Evaluation (CNE) to oversee quality assurance within institutions. CNE, an independent body set up by Act of Parliament in 1985, was mandated to evaluate higher education establishments and the value of the public service tasks that they provide (Staropoli 1991; Neave 1991).

In Australia, interest in quality in higher education also emerged in the mid-1980s. A Green Paper from 1985 stated that 'financial discretion in the hands of the institutions must be balanced with accountability'. It made it clear that funding would be allocated on output and performance with 'funding based in part on performance measures'. Institutions were asked to consider appropriate funding-linked indicators (Teather 1990). The subsequent White Paper (1988) Higher Education, A Policy Statement introduced a new funding mechanism and removed the binary divide between universities and colleges of advanced education.

The United States of America (USA), with its federal system and mixed public and private higher education sector, also expressed official concern about the quality of higher education. In the past, academics had expressed concerns about the standards of courses but, by the mid-1980s, government groups were taking an interest (Millard 1991). The National Institute of Education (SGCEAHE 1984) report Involvement in Learning: Realising the Potential of American Higher Education called for greater student involvement in the learning process and for more focus on the outcomes of the process.

In the USA, individual states are responsible for their own planning and funding and they have responded to the quality and standards concerns in a various ways, including the introduction of state-wide and state-mandated tests, more stringent entry requirements, financial incentives for curriculum innovation and outcomes assessment and linking state funding to institutional outcomes performance.

Germany has been the one country in Europe that has significantly resisted the headlong rush to external quality monitoring. Despite reported public concerns about the quality of German higher education in the mid-1980s, notably the duration of studies (which has been higher in Germany than most other European countries) and concern about the quality of teaching and learning, there has been little progress on the imposition of external review. The federal system and the legal constitution of universities has meant that Länder ministers for education have done little more than exert gentle pressure on the institutions to sort the problems out for themselves.

Thus, it has been evident from the start that quality has been used as a vehicle for delivering policy requirements within available resources. On the one hand, it operates as a mechanism to encourage change but it also operates to legitimate policy-driven change, which includes making higher education more relevant to social and economic needs, widening access, expanding numbers and usually doing it with a decreasing unit cost. External quality monitoring (EQM) became the predominant operational mechanism through which quality is used to legitimate policy (Harvey & Knight 1996).

THE DEVOLUTION OF ACCOUNTABILITY

Degree of government control, extent of devolved responsibility, funding systems and the overall structure and internal organisation of higher education vary from one country to the next. Nonetheless there has been a convergence in all systems towards a dominant model of delegated accountability using a fairly standardised review methodology (Figure 1). The systems that have traditionally espoused a market approach and those that have been influenced by the traditional British system of autonomous institutions supported by the state are finding their autonomy being eroded by government-backed requirements to demonstrate accountability and value for money (Bauer and Kogan 1995). Where central control was, or continues to be, exerted over higher education, for example in China, Eastern Europe, South America and Scandinavia, there has been increasing delegated responsibility for quality but at the price of being required to be accountable and open to scrutiny. Thus, in those countries where a new accountable autonomy is being granted, self-assessment is seen as indicative of the shift to self-governance. In those countries where universities have traditionally been autonomous, self-evaluation is seen as not only politically pragmatic but a necessary vehicle to ensure the institution focuses its attention on quality issues.

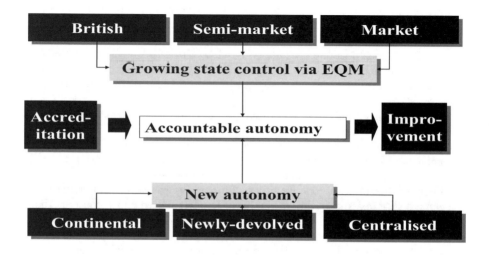

Figure 1. Delegated accountability (adapted from Harvey and Knight, 1996).

The convergence to accountable autonomy is reflected in a widespread methodology. Most EQM agencies make use of various combinations of three basic data collection tools, self-assessment, peer review and performance indicators, followed by a public report, usually containing recommendations (Green and Harvey 1994; Frazer 1995).

The widespread use of this approach is as much about political pragmatism as it is about the efficacy of the research methodology, or improvement impact. In those countries where a new accountable autonomy is being granted, self-assessment is seen as indicative of the shift to self-governance. In those settings where universities have traditionally been autonomous, or academics have been free from close scrutiny, self-evaluation is seen as necessary to lessen the 'inspectorial' element of review. A process of self-evaluation 'checked' by peer review in one way or another is the norm in countries as diverse as the USA, Brazil, Britain, Netherlands, Norway, Portugal, Australia, South Africa, and China. In most countries self-evaluation, while guided by an indicative framework, is mediated by reference to the mission of the institution, to allow for diversity within the system. Peer review usually includes a visit by a group of 'respected' academic peers to the institution being evaluated. Most countries outside the British Isles have not included direct observation of the teaching situation as part of peer evaluation.

PURPOSES OF QUALITY MONITORING

External monitoring has a variety of objects of attention, foci and purposes. For example, the main object of the quality monitoring process may be the provider, which tends to be the case with institutional review. However, attention may be on the output of a programme of study or the medium of delivery, especially if the programme is delivered unconventionally. In some instances the learner rather than the provider may be the primary object of the review, although this is not common (Figure 2).

The focus may or may not be confined to the learning interface or it may encompass the governance and regulation of an institution. If the focus is on the learning, it might be directed at the curriculum, particularly design, organisation, assessment, support and learning infrastructure. Alternatively, the focus might be on the learner, rather than the programme, or simply on the validity of the qualification, as tends to be the case in some professional accreditation of programmes.

There are a variety of specific purposes of quality monitoring, which fall under four broad headings: accountability, control, compliance and improvement. (Figure 2):

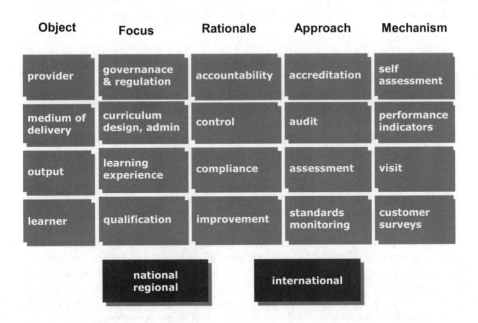

Figure 2. Object, focus, rationale, approach and mechanisms for external evaluation.

Accountability

Accountability has been the dominant underlying rationale for introducing quality evaluation. In countries where university autonomy is traditional or based on the market, there has been a growing demand for explicit accountability. Conversely, in countries where higher education has been controlled, accountability is the price of increased autonomy. Accountability is required because of the cost of massification, the need to account for and prioritise public expenditure and hence the pressure to ensure value for both private and public monies. There is also a more general pressure; to identify clear lines of accountability within higher education systems.

A second aspect of accountability is to students: assurance that the programme of study is organised and run properly and that an appropriate educational experience is both promised and delivered. In some cases, quality evaluation aims to ensure that students receive comparable 'service' — quantity and quality of teaching, study facilities, learning support, pastoral support, equality of opportunity and so on. Evaluations can be used to monitor whether students are getting the level of service that they have been promised or a minimum national level of service.

A third accountability purpose is the generation of public information about the quality of institutions and programmes. This might be information for funders that can be used, for example, to aid funding allocation decisions. It may be information for users, such as prospective students and graduate recruiters, that helps inform choice. However, to date, there is little evidence to suggest that students or employers make much use of information that results from quality monitoring evaluations.

Control

There are two elements to the control function of quality. First, is the desire of governments to control the higher education system in various ways, such as to restrict unrestrained growth, which is often done via financial controls but which also now includes using the outcomes of quality monitoring to encourage or restrict expansion.

Second, is a more generic control of the status and standing of higher education. External review is used to ensure that the principles and practices of higher education are not being eroded or flouted, thereby undermining the intrinsic quality of university-level education and research. Globalisation and the internationalisation of higher education, new forms of delivery and an increasingly unrestricted market are all features of a landscape that seems to be out of control. This has resulted in international as well as national attempts to control higher education.

The control aspect of quality evaluation specifically addresses the comparability of standards, that is the standard or level of student academic or professional achievement, nationally and internationally. Attempts have been made to 'benchmark' academic standards including: externally set and marked examinations; specification of the content of syllabuses; (threshold) descriptors of outcomes; external examiners to ensure inter-institutional comparability of awards. The use of external examiners, for example, is well established in some countries as a means of making comparisons between programmes within subject disciplines.

Compliance

External quality monitoring also encourages compliance to emerging or existing government policy. There is growing governmental pressure for the university sector to be more responsive to value-for-money concerns, more relevant to social and economic needs, and engage in widening access. In addition there is pressure to ensure comparability of provision and procedures, within and between institutions, including international comparisons.

There are other stakeholders who seek compliance through quality monitoring, notably professional or regulatory bodies who may use quality monitoring to check that their preferences or policies are being acknowledged or implemented.

At its simplest level, quality monitoring has encouraged, or even forced, compliance in the production of information, be it statistical data, prospectuses, or course documents. Such compliance means that taken-for-granted practices and procedures have had to be confronted and clearly documented. 'It represents the minimum required shift from an entirely producer-oriented approach to higher education to one that acknowledges the rights of other stakeholders to minimum information and a degree of "service".' (Harvey 1998: 241).

Improvement

Most systems of external review claim to encourage improvement. Despite the rhetoric, improvement has been a secondary feature of most systems, especially when first established. In some rare cases, such as the Swedish audits, improvement was designed in from the outset through the identification of improvement projects and evaluating their effectiveness. Compliance and accountability have been the dominant purposes and any improvement element has been secondary. As systems move into second or third phases, the improvement element has been given more attention (Figure 1).

The most effective improvement occurs when external processes mesh with internal improvement activities. In the main, external processes tend to effect improvement at the organisational level and may encourage better use of and investment in infrastructure. It is more difficult for external review to engage with the learning-teaching interface. In essence, quality review should encourage continuous improvement of the learning and teaching process, but evidence to date suggests otherwise.

The improvement function of quality monitoring procedures is to encourage institutions to reflect upon their practices and to develop what they do. Evaluation needs to be designed to encourage a process of continuous improvement of the learning process and the range of outcomes. Arguably, the assessment of value-added is at the core of any improvement-oriented, value-for-money and transformative approach to quality.

DIFFERENT FORMS FOR DIFFERENT PURPOSES

External quality monitoring takes several forms, ranging from accreditation and institutional audit, through subject assessment and standards monitoring to customer surveys. They have varied objects, foci and purposes and relate to different notions of quality and standards.

Accreditation

Accreditation is the establishment or revalidation of the status, legitimacy or appropriateness of an institution, programme (i.e. composite of modules) or module of study. It has been described as a public statement that a certain threshold of quality is passed (Campbell et al. 2000; Kristoffersen, Sursock & Westerheijden 1998). The formal public recognition embodied in accreditation is seen as being based on agreed, pre-defined standards or criteria (El-Khawas 1998; Sursock 2000). Accreditation, thus has two nuances: first, the 'abstract notion of a formal authorising power', enacted via official decisions about recognition and, second, the quality label that institutions or programmes may acquire through certain accreditation procedures' (Haakstad 2001: 77). Accreditation is thus of an institution or of a programme of study. Programme accreditation may be academic accreditation or professional accreditation, that is, accreditation of professional competence to practice. Accreditation is a binary state, either a programme or an institution is accredited, or it is not (Haakstad 2001: 77).
Accreditation tends to focus on inputs such as resources, curricula and staffing. Sometimes it addresses the teaching process but rarely explores outcomes such as the graduate abilities and employability. The exceptions are some of the professional programme accreditations undertaken in the UK or US (Harvey & Mason 1995; Westerheijden 2001).

In principal, rather than the input-process-output focus, accreditation might be based on recognition that the institution has in place appropriate control and monitoring processes to ensure satisfactory quality and standards. However, identifying appropriate mechanisms is normally viewed as an auditing function (see below) distinct from, but possibly contributing to, a formal process of accreditation of an institution. The same approach could, if the audit is subject focussed, also be used to validate or accredit programmes.

At the institutional level, accreditation effectively provides a licence to operate. It is usually based on an evaluation of whether the institution meets specified minimum (input) standards such as staff qualifications, research activities, student intake and learning resources. It might also be based on an estimation of the potential for the institution to produce graduates that meet explicit or implicit academic standard or professional competence. In Europe, institutional accreditation or revalidation is usually undertaken by national bodies, either government departments or government-initiated agencies or quangos that make formal judgements on recognition. In the United States, accreditation is a self-regulatory process of recognition of institutional viability by non-governmental regional voluntary associations (Petersen 1995). Institutional accreditation, especially initial recognition, tends to be more prominent in countries with a significant private higher education provision, such as those in the Americas and Eastern Europe.

Audit

Audit is the process of checking to ensure externally- or internally-specified practices and procedures are in place. Audits might establish the existence of such procedures or may attempt to audit their effectiveness. Audit might be of specific aspects of provision but is usually pitched at an institutional level.

Normally, audits check whether procedures are in place to assure quality or standards of higher education. This usually requires an institution to specify its internal quality-monitoring procedures, including identification of responsibilities and intra-institutional communication and co-ordination of practices. Audits do not usually attempt to evaluate the institution as such, just to ensure that the institution has clearly-defined internal quality monitoring procedures linked to effective action. This approach, which probably started in Britain (HEQC DQA 1993), has been developed in New Zealand (NZUAAU 1997) and Sweden (NAHE 1996; 1997), and is often considered as having the potential of meeting many of the expectations of external control at the same time as it might support improvement (Dill 2000). In Sweden, the approach to audit undertaken by the National Agency was to focus on the stated improvement agendas of institutions and explore the efficacy of improvement projects and the approach appears to have aided the development of quality awareness and quality work in the institutions, taking the notion of 'the learning organisation' as its point of departure (Askling 1997; 1998).

The current proposal in the UK is to strengthen audit by enabling it to 'drill-down', that is, take a closer look at specific aspects of audit or particular areas where audit might suggest anomalies (QAA 2002). This is very similar to drilling down in financial auditing.

Assessment

Quality assessments set out to measure the level of quality of inputs, processes and, sometimes, outputs. This may be a judgment of the overall quality of an institution or programme or of specified component elements. In France, for example, the Comité National d'Évaluation (CNE) evaluates each institution holistically (Staropoli 1991; Ribier 1995).[1] Measurement may be against externally-set criteria (both implicit and explicit), against internally-specified objectives or missions, or a mutually agreed set of criteria. Many assessments are supposedly of fitness for purpose and thus institutions or programmes are assessed against mission-based criteria. In practice, there is a set of overarching expectations and the mission-based variability operates within narrow tolerances. Assessment might include a complex grading system or might be based on a simple satisfactory/non-satisfactory dichotomy.

Assessment may also 'benchmark'[2] against other institutions, national norms or against oneself over time. Benchmarks tend to be quantifiable and restricted to measurable items, including the presence or absence of an element of service or a facility. Currently, benchmarking tends to be a voluntary activity engaged in by institutions.

Assessment may focus on inputs (such as teaching staff, learning resources) or process (such as teaching, learning, support services) or outcomes (such as students academic standards of achievement or professional competence, employment rates, student perception of their learning). Assessment evidence includes statistical indicators, observation, direct evaluation of research outputs, student and graduate views, employer views, student performance, self-assessment and other documentation, discussion and interviews with teachers, students and managers, and perceptions of other agencies, such as professional bodies.

Standards monitoring

In systems that have made use of external examiners, external monitoring of standards predates external quality monitoring by many years. External examiners are, or have been, used to monitor standards on postgraduate or undergraduate degrees in the UK, Denmark, Ireland, New Zealand, Malaysia, Brunei, India, Malawi, Hong Kong and in the technikons in South Africa (Silver 1993; Warren Piper 1994). In some professional areas, the external control on standards by regulatory or professional bodies has been a much more important factor than quality monitoring as the former is often linked to professional accreditation and the awarding of a licence to practice.

Standards monitoring has two main focuses: first, academic standards of a programme of study, identified by the academic work produced by students; second, standards of professional competence identified through the ability or potential to undertake professional practice.

Standards monitoring may specify standards that are appropriate or it may endeavour to ensure that standards are at appropriate levels, possibly by checking or even grading student work or performance. Standards monitoring may also attempt to ensure comparability of standards across the sector or across specific subject disciplines. External examiners inevitably make comparisons between programmes within subject disciplines, even if it is based on limited experience. Sometimes they grade directly but usually standards are inferred by scrutiny of a sample of work or by monitoring award statistics. Where there are, for example, externally-set and marked examinations, this can also be used to compare (or benchmark) standards. Some professional bodies in the UK set examinations linked to recognition of practice (Harvey & Mason 1995) and the *provão* in Brazil is an example of subject-based national examination designed to monitor standards.

A further purpose of standards monitoring is to enable the development of national and international systems of credit accumulation and transfer. Credit accumulation and transfer (CAT) has been in place in some countries for many years and is designed to ensure flexibility and responsiveness to student requirements and increased mobility. However, few students really take advantage of CAT schemes beyond the crediting of a single term or semester of study as an exchange student with a recognised partner institution or via a formal programme, such as ERASMUS in the EU. Furthermore, many CAT schemes function better in theory than they do when put to practical test and some students can find themselves disadvantaged when using them as they find that aspects of their study are not acknowledged.

Customer surveys

Sometimes quality review includes participant or 'client' satisfaction with service provision (at institutional, programme or module level), in which case feedback from students, graduates or employers enhance the normal process of self-assessment, statistical indicators and peer review, as, for example, in the assessments made by the

Danish Centre for Quality Assurance and Evaluation of Higher Education (Thune 1993).[3] Measurement of 'customer' opinions (satisfaction) such as the Student Satisfaction Survey at UCE (Harvey, 2001) and the Student Barometer at Lund University (Lund University 1997) are used as annual indicators of service provision and inform management decision-making.

IMPACT OF QUALITY MONITORING

The exposé of different external monitoring procedures in previous sections indicate that the quality issue affects the institutions in many ways. Thus, external monitoring, in itself a response to changes that are exerting great direct and indirect impact on institutions, may act as catalysts rather than having a direct impact (Askling 1997).

Devolution of authority, new missions and obligations, new categories of students are changes that have contributed to the governments' keen interest in evaluation and monitoring and have evidently, irrespective of the introduction of evaluation and monitoring, introduced new tasks and also framed the space of action for institutions and their staff.

New Public Management and self-regulation, as alternatives to former models of state regulation, have brought about an array of normative models of institutional governance such as corporate enterprise, entrepreneurial university, adaptive university and learning university. The models are examples of efforts to find a proper balance between internal (academic) influence and external (corporate or market dominated) influences, between organisational stability and flexibility, all in order to maximise the capacity for institutional development within a frame of state control. In all of them, quality monitoring plays an important role (Askling & Henkel 1988).

In many countries, the institutional leadership has strengthened and the qualifications required for strategic academic leadership are identified. Universities today are complex organisations in a period of constant change and need leaders who can turn complexity into meaning by providing sense and transparency in situations characterised by confusion (Askling & Stensaker 2002). The internal 'architecture' of institutions and also the relative balance between providers, sponsors and clients must, it is argued, be taken into account when forming the expectations on academic leadership and institutional management (Middlehurst 1999).

A more pronounced task differentiation in universities and the development of a new collegiality are logical consequences when the quality of students' learning experiences are threatened by increase in student number, decline in funding and the array of additional tasks (Elton 1996). New ways of learning in higher education have been explored (Bowden & Marton 1998; Elton 1996; 1999) and there is a growing concern about university teachers' professional development and their responsibility for quality in learning and knowledge production. The establishment of centres for teaching and learning, and the allocation of special funding for improvement-oriented developmental work, are two measures that have been taken in many countries on a national level or by individual institutions.

Experiences tell us that student learning is mostly affected by curriculum, organisation and technological change but this is itself more directly affected by professional bodies, teacher development and integrating new forms of communication and flexible course structure, which in turn are more likely to be market driven than initiated as a result of quality assurance. In effect, it seems that quality monitoring is bringing up the rear, checking on changes rather than being a major factor in change.

Delegates at The End of Quality? international seminar in Birmingham 2002 expressed considerable doubt about the efficiency of most external quality monitoring.

> Apart from the excessive cost to the exchequer of external systems, the internal costs of monitoring, in some countries, are enormous and in no way reflect the value gained from the process. Not only does external quality monitoring fail, in many systems, to engage with the internal improvement, its periodic and dramaturgical manifestations do not readily help inform change management in institutions. (Harvey 2002).

Furthermore, Westerheijden (2001), for example, argues that national accreditation arrangements work towards national uniformity rather than diversity. External quality monitoring actually inhibits innovation because of the application of conservative or rigid evaluation criteria. Impact of monitoring leads to uniformity and not to diversity and flexibility.

More damaging than lack of innovation and conformity, is the temporary rather than permanent nature of review-inspired improvements. There is considerable anecdotal evidence that the initial impact fades away quickly, especially if there is no significant connection between internal and external processes. External monitoring must interact with internal quality systems: the real benefits are products of the external-internal dialogue. The issue is how to embed changes that result from quality monitoring processes. The more the process is one of complying with external requirements the less the lasting internal benefits. This whole process is exacerbated by links to funding, which drives institutions to conceal weaknesses rather than engage in self-evaluation and improvement.

Copenhagen Business School is an example of an institution that has changed dramatically in a decade from a didactic teaching institution to a learning-oriented university (Kristensen 1997). There has been a significant cultural change but this has been facilitated by physical changes including new buildings and new technology, changes to course organisation linked to changing student numbers and finance, committed and secure senior management with vision and energy to drive internal changes, and a new generation of innovative staff. External quality monitoring has had some role in this, but in rather complex ways.

Thus, there is little or no evidence of clear impact of quality monitoring on learning (Harvey 2002). The structure and organisation of external quality monitoring is not compatible with empowering staff and students to enhance the learning situation. Indeed, research suggests that other factors entirely outweigh the impact of external quality monitoring on student learning. Horsburgh, (1998: 23) for example, mapped the dialectical interrelationship between the factors that impact on degree programmes and the student experience of learning. She suggests that there are far more important factors impacting on innovation in learning than external quality monitoring.

CONCLUSION

External quality monitoring of higher education has grown throughout the 1990s. Yet, while experience grows, there is no commensurate growth in evaluation of the impact of monitoring quality. On the contrary, evaluation of all these external monitoring procedures, mentioned in this chapter, appears to be a rather ad hoc process. In many countries, governments have introduced and changed models of external quality monitoring without have anything else that value-loaded expectations as ground for their decisions.

One obvious reason is that there been considerable change in the higher education over the last decade driven by factors other than quality monitoring. Technological changes, massification, pressure for closer links to employment, general reduction in funding per head and internationalisation have been far more significant than quality review.

However, whether an example of impact or not, internal quality work has mushroomed. Individual researchers within the research fields of teaching and learning and didactics have inspired each others and also challenged university teachers to make powerful contributions to improve university teaching. In many cases they have also paved the way for the establishment of centres of teaching and learning. The have contributed in turning the quality issue, originally imposed by governments, into something that apparently is empowering teachers and students.

We agree with the delegates at The End of Quality? seminar, in arguing that the primary purpose of quality monitoring bureaucracies should be to act as catalysts for internal improvement within institutions. This role requires dialogue and advice as part of the monitoring procedure and the renewal of a trusting relationship between external body and institutions. There must be an emphasis on dialogue and support in EQM to give room for continuous improvement and process-driven quality improvements. Such processes will generate their own performance indicators, which will be owned by institutions and will measure real improvement (Harvey 2002).

NOTES

[1] CNE does not in any way accredit the institution.

[2] Benchmarking is, currently, a widely applied term although its use is far from consistent. The use by QAA in Britain is closer to the specification of a national curriculum than it is to the notion of direct comparative measurement.

[3] The Danish Centre for Quality Assurance and Evaluation of Higher Education is now part of the Danish Evaluation Institute with a broader brief.

REFERENCES

Askling, B. (1997). 'Quality monitoring as an institutional enterprise', *Quality in Higher Education*, 3(1), 17–26.

Askling, B. (1998). *Quality Work in Swedish Universities in a Period of Transformation* (Report No. 1998:04). (Göteborg; Dept. of Education and Educational Research, Göteborg University).

Askling, B. & Henkel, M. (1988). Higher education institutions. In Kogan, M, Marianne Bauer, Ivar Bleiklie and Mary Henkel (1988). *Transforming Higher Education. A Comparative Study.* London: Jessica Kingsley Publishers.

Askling, B. & Stensaker, B. (2002). Academic Leadership: prescriptions, practices and paradoxes. *Tertiary Education and Management* 8(2), 113–125.

Bauer, M. & Kogan, M. (1995). 'Evaluation systems in the UK and Sweden: Successes and difficulties', paper for the the *Conference on 'Evaluating Universities'*, AF-Forum, Rome, 26–27 September, 1995.

Bleiklie, I. (1998). Justifying the evaluative state: New Public Management ideals in higher education. *European Journal of Education.* 33(3), 299–316.

Bowden, J. & Marton, F. (1998). *The University of Learning. Beyond Quality and Competence in Higher Education.* London: Kogan Page.

Campbell, C., Kanaan, S., Kehm, B., Mockiene, B., Westerheijden, D. F., & Williams, R. (2000). *The European University: A handbook on institutional approaches to strategic management, quality management, European policy and academic recognition.* Torino: European Training Foundation.

Committee of Vice-Chancellors and Principals of the Universities of the United Kingdom (CVCP) (1985). *Report of the Steering Committee for Efficiency Studies in Universities.* (The Jarratt Report). London, CVCP.

Department of Education and Science (DES) (1985). *Development of Higher Education into the 1990s*, Green Paper, Cmnd. 9524. London, HMSO.

Dill, D. (2000). 'Designing academic audit: lessons learned in Europe and Asia' *Quality in Higher Education*, 6(3), 186–207.

Eaton, J. (2001). *Circular letter*, 6 December, 2001.

El-Khawas, E. (1998). 'Accreditation's role in quality assurance in the United States' *Higher Education Management*, 10(3), 43–56

Elton, L. (1996). Task differentiation in Universities: Towards a New Collegiality. *Tertiary Education and Management*, 2(2), 138–145.

Elton, L. (1999). New ways of learning in higher education: managing the change. *Tertiary Education and Management*, 5(3), 207–225.

Frazer, M. (1995). 'Ten papers on national developments', in International Network of Quality Assurance Agencies in Higher Education (INQAAHE), 1995, *Third Meeting of the INQAAHE, 21–23 May 1995, Utrecht, the Netherlands: Proceedings* (pp. 55-71). The Netherlands, VSNU/IHO/INQAAHE.

Goedegebuure, L.C.J., Maassen, P.A.M. & Westerheijden, D.F. (Eds.) (1990). *Peer Review and Performance Indicators: Quality Assessment in British and Dutch Higher Education*. Culemborg: Lemma.

Green, D. & Harvey, L. (1994). 'Quality assurance in Western Europe: trends, practices and issues', in Banta,T., Anderson, C. and Berendt, B, (Ed.), 1994, *Proceedings of the Fifth International Conference on Assessing Quality in Higher Education* (pp. 177-200) Indianapolis, Indiana University-Purdue University.

Haakstad, J. (2001). 'Accreditation : the new quality assurance formula? Some reflections as Norway is about to reform its quality assurance system', *Quality in Higher Education*, 77–82.

Harvey, L. & Knight, P. (1996). *Transforming Higher Education*. Buckingham, Open University Press and Society for Research into Higher Education.

Harvey, L. & Mason, S. (1995). *The Role of Professional Bodies in Higher education Quality Monitoring*. Birmingham: QHE.

Harvey, L. (1998). 'An assessment of past and current approaches to quality in higher education', *Australian Journal of Education*, 42(3), 237–55

Harvey, L. (2001). *The 2001 Report on the Student Experience at UCE*. Birmingham, Centre for Research into Quality, University of Central England in Birmingham.

Harvey, L. (2002). 'The End of Quality', *Quality in Higher Education*, 8(1). An earlier version can be found on http://www.qualityresearchinternational.com.

Higher Education Quality Council, Division of Quality Audit (HEQC DQA) (1993). *Notes for Guidance of Auditors*, January. Birmingham: HEQC.

Horsburgh, M. (1998). Quality Monitoring in Higher Education: A Case Study of the Impact on Student Learning, Unpublished doctoral thesis, Charles Sturt University.

Kristensen, B. (1997). The impact of quality monitoring on institutions: A Danish experience at the Copenhagen Business School. Quality in Higher Education, 3(1), 87–94.

Kristoffersen, D., Sursock, A. & Westerheijden, D. F. (1998). *Manual of Quality Assurance: Procedures and Practice*. Torino: European Training Foundation.

Middlehurst, R. (1999). New realities for leadership and governance in higher education? *Tertiary Education and Management*. 5(4), 307 – 329.

Millard, R. M. (1991). 'Governance, Quality and Equity in the United States' in Berdahl, R. O., Moodie, G. C., Spitzberg Jr, I. J. (Eds.) (1991). *Quality and Access in Higher Education - Comparing Britain and the United States*, Buckingham, SRHE and the Open University Press, 58–74.

Ministry for Education and Science (Dutch) (1985). Hoger Onderwijs, Autonomie en Kwaliteit [Higher Education, Autonomy and Quality], Den Haag, SDU.

National Agency for Higher Education (NAHE) (1996). *Quality Assurance as Support for Processes of Innovation: The Swedish model in comparative perspective*. Stockholm, NAHE.

Lund University (1997). *Studentbarometern: Resultatredovisning*. Rapport nr 97:200. Lund, Lund University.

National Agency for Higher Education (NAHE) (1997). *The National Quality Audit of Higher Education in Sweden*. Stockholm, NAHE.

Neave, M. (1991). Models of Quality Assurance in Europe, London, CNAA.

New Zealand Universities Academic Audit Unit (NZUAAU) (1997). *Report of a Review of New Zealand Universities Academic Audit Unit*. Wellington, UAAU.

Study Group on the Conditions of Excellence in American Higher Education (SGCEAHE) (1984). *Involvement in Learning: Realising the Potential of American Higher Education*, Washington, D.C., National Institute for Higher Education.

Petersen, J. C. (1995). 'Report proposes accreditation changes in US', *QA*, 8: 6–7, February.

Pollitt, C. (1993) *Managerialism and the Public Services. The Anglo-American Experiences*. Oxford: Basil Blackwell.

Quality Assurance Agency for Higher Education (QAA) (2002) website http://www.qaa.ac.uk.

Ribier, R. (1995). 'The role of governments vis-à-vis the evaluation agencies'. In: *Background Papers for the Third Meeting of the International Network of Quality Assurance Agencies in Higher Education* (INQAAHE), pp. 214-215, Utrecht, The Netherlands, 21–23 May 1995, VSNU/Inspectorate of Education.

Silver, H. (1993). *External Examiners: Changing Roles?* London: CNAA.

Staropoli, A. (1991). 'Quality assurance in France', paper presented to the Hong Kong Council for Academic Accreditation *Conference on 'Quality Assurance in Higher Education'*, Hong Kong, 15–17 July.

Sursock, A. (2000). 'Towards accreditation schemes for higher education in Europe?', paper at *CRE workshop*, 8–9 Nov. 2000, Vienna.

Teather, D. (1990). 'Performance indicators in Australian higher education: the context and an appraisal of the 1988 report' in Dochy, F. J. R. C, Segers, M. S. R, Wijnen, W. H. F. W. (eds.), *Management Information and Performance Indicators in Higher Education: an International Issue* (pp. 103-118). Van Gorcum, Assen/Maastricht.

Thune, C. (1993). 'The experience with establishing procedures for evaluation and quality assurance of higher education in Denmark', paper presented at the *First Biennial Conference and General Conference of the International Network of Quality Assurance Agencies in Higher Education*, Montréal, Canada, 24–28 May 1993.

Warren Piper, D. J. (1994). *Are Professors Professional? The organisation of university examinations*. London: Jessica Kingsley.

Westerheijden, D.F. (2001). '*Ex oriente lux*?: national and multiple accreditation in Europe after the fall of the Wall and after Bologna', *Quality in Higher Education*, 7(1), 65–76.

Commonwealth of Australia (1988). *Higher Education, A Policy Statement*. White Paper. Canberra. Australian Government Publishing Service.

PETER MAASSEN AND BJØRN STENSAKER

INTERPRETATIONS OF SELF-REGULATION:

THE CHANGING STATE-HIGHER EDUCATION
RELATIONSHIP IN EUROPE

Abstract. Especially in Continental Europe, the concept of self-regulation has, during the last 20 years, played an important role in the political thinking with respect to higher education. As such it has provided the foundation for numerous changes in the state–higher education relationship. In this chapter various formal interpretations of 'self-regulation', as used in higher education reform processes, are presented. However, in the practice of higher education, the efforts to introduce a 'self-regulation' steering approach often resulted in divergent and partly contradictory governance and steering arrangements. Referring to these experiences, the authors point to the importance of the symbolic nature of the 'self-regulation' reforms, and more generally, to the symbolic dimension in policy processes that should receive more attention in the analyses of changes in the state–higher education relationships in Europe, as elsewhere.

INTRODUCTION

Throughout the 1980s, higher education in Europe underwent many far-reaching changes. An extensive growth in student numbers all over Europe, a relative decrease in public investment in higher education, and the need to revitalise higher education to the needs of a more research-intensive business and industry sector, were only some of the many factors that made it necessary to look at the relationship between the state and higher education in new ways.

One of the most influential ideas on how public policy could respond to these changes was the concept of self-regulation, that emerged in higher education in the late 1980s (Van Vught 1989). As an alternative to the then dominating idea of central planning and control, self-regulation spread rapidly as the basis for numerous reform initiatives in higher education (see e.g. Neave & Van Vught 1991; Maassen & Van Vught 1996). Self-regulation postulated the need to emphasise the capacities of the decentralised decision-making units, as well as the need to identify and monitor a critical number of feedback variables and performance recipes (Van Vught 1989: 37-39). As such, the concept can be said to acknowledge the ideas of 'bounded rationality' in organisation studies, thereby doing justice to the increasing complexity and uncertainty higher education faced in this period.

The governmental lack of firm knowledge concerning the basic activities of higher education institutions was one of the main reasons for the interest in the concept. As one of the national governments involved indicated, the then steering model with respect to higher education was not effective enough, and self-regulation offered an alternative model that was expected to lead to a more effective governmental steering of higher education (Maassen & Van Vught 1989).

In this chapter, we shall take a closer look at the self-regulation concept. A starting point for our discussion is the symbolic dimension of the introduction of the self-regulation concept in higher education. We shall attempt to identify the reasons for the attractiveness of the concept, and the ways in which it was interpreted and applied in

R. Begg (ed.), The Dialogue between Higher Education Research and Practice, 85–95.

various policy contexts. In the conclusion, we argue that the symbolic nature of the concept is an important factor in understanding its diffusion, and that the symbolic nature of policy ideas and concepts are important sources for also analysing current changes in the state–higher education relationship.

SELF-REGULATION: STEERING THROUGH INFORMATION

The theoretical roots of the concept of self-regulation can be found in cybernetics (see for example, Van Vught 1989). Some of the ambiguities related to the application of the self-regulation concept in higher education can be traced back to its cybernetic origins.

The first issue concerns the basic nature of self-regulation: Is it a policy objective in its own right or a governmental steering strategy? Going back to the founders of cybernetics provides us with a somewhat ambiguous answer. Parsons (1995: 368), for example, argues that Karl Deutsch, one of the founders of cybernetics, indeed had a prescriptive motive for his model of peaceful coexistence between the governed and those who govern, emphasising that learning and mutual adjustments would take place in both camps. Even if several authors in higher education have emphasised that self-regulation should, first and foremost, be understood as a steering strategy (see: Van Vught 1989; Neave & Van Vught 1991), it is tempting to argue that the possibility to interpret 'self-regulation' and 'increased institutional autonomy' as an end in itself, and not only as a means to steer higher education, was an attractive idea for several authors (see, for example, Kells 1992; Barnett 1993).

A second issue is the role of the various actors in a self-regulatory system. What is, for example, the role of the government in such a system? Parsons (1995: 367) argues that in some versions of cybernetic models, amongst others in Deutsch's model, there seems to be a preference for a rather prominent government role, emphasising 'enforceable decisions' and active governmental steering. However, Parsons also notes that Deutsch warned against extensive use of power by governments. Governmental decision-making should not be 'power engineering' and the society should, in an ideal situation, be a 'self-steering' entity. This ambiguity with respect to the role of the government can also be found in discussions about self-regulation in higher education. Van Vught (1996: 193) argues, for example, that self-regulation and governmental steering form in some respects an incompatible combination, since governmental steering is in principle contradictory to self-regulation, as self-regulation implies that a system has its own feedback loops and control capacity. This would mean that in higher education the universities and colleges themselves are responsible for monitoring input, processes and output, and that, in such a system, governments do not have a 'natural' place. According to Van Vught (1996) governments should only act as a second-order regulator, responsible for managing the rules of the game, and not the game itself.

In a book on self-regulation strategies in the field of quality assurance, Kells (1992: 41) pointed out that, even if he supported the idea of self-regulation, there was 'certainly a formidable set of technical and potentially influential attitudinal barriers to the effective functioning of a self-regulation system'. Thus, not only did he argue strongly for the responsibility of the individual institution in this process, Kells, indirectly, also puts a lot of responsibility on the side of the government, claiming that self-regulating institutions are the positive result of a well developed and balanced self-regulation steering strategy by national authorities (Kells 1992: 35-38). Accordingly, he seemed to interpret the role of government in higher education as being both the first- and second-order regulator.

An interesting twist concerning the role of government also occurs if one compares how the self-regulation concept was defined in Europe and in the USA. In European higher education, self-regulation was a concept that referred to system level governance with little weight given to the consequences for institutional leadership, management and administration. In the USA, the situation was almost the opposite, in the sense that there was hardly any interest in conceptualising state level governance with the help of cybernetics, while a number of interesting applications of cybernetics in the area of institutional leadership and management were made. The most prominent examples of the latter can be found in Birnbaum's work, especially in his seminal book How Colleges Work (Birnbaum 1989).

A third issue, when going back to the foundations of cybernetics, is related to the policy instruments opted for. What policy tools are compatible with a self-regulation approach? Deutsch (1963: 182) seemed at first to be firm and decisive on this issue, when he argued that information and communications engineering should be the focus of governmental inference. Those to be governed would learn by feedback. They would react to forecasts about the consequences of decisions and actions. Governmental action should be concentrated on the control of information flows and the 'steering' of the feedback. However, when examining the various feedback modes by Deutsch more closely, one could argue that a variety of policy tools is compatible with self-regulation. Giving the governed 'negative feedback' creates, for example, an opening for using the means of laws and regulations rather than only information. Early observers of empirical changes in the state-higher education relationship have come to a similar conclusion, interpreting self-regulation tendencies by governments in some European countries as 'de-regulation' more than applying various information tools (see, for example, Aamodt et al. 1991). It is interesting to note that the later development of various national evaluation systems is often interpreted as a form of 're-regulating' higher education, and not as an element in the implementation of a more self-regulatory system by 'enhancing the information flow and the 'feedback' loops of the system, for stimulating the system capacity to foresee change, or as necessary forecasts about the needs for future (self-regulative) action' (cf. Deutsch 1963: 188-189).

Thus, one might conclude that the idea of self-regulation rested on a cybernetic perspective that was not very distinct and perhaps not very applicable in the real world 'in which conflict over goals and how they can be measured is the stuff of governments and politics' (Parsons 1995: 368). As a consequence, it is perhaps not surprising that the introduction of the self-regulation concept in higher education was associated with much confusion and what seemed to be conflicting interests (Neave & Van Vught 1991: 250-251; see also Reed, Meek & Jones 2002).

THE DIFFUSION OF SELF-REGULATION AS A (SYMBOLIC) POLICY IDEA

If we accept that self-regulation was a much less clear and distinct steering strategy than initially acclaimed, it can be asked how the spread of this steering strategy to so many corners of Europe can be explained. We believe that part of the explanation can be found in the symbolic attractiveness of the self-regulation concept, referring both to the characteristics of the concept as such, as well as to the political context in which it was introduced.

Important characteristics of self-regulation can, for example, be related to institutionalised notions about what 'proper' policy ideas should look like (Meyer 1996). Echoing recent reflections by the political scientist, Christopher Hood, one might say that 'shifts in what counts as received ideas in public management works through a process of fashion and persuasion, not through proofs couched in a strict deductive logic, controlled experiments, or even systematic analysis of available cases' (Hood 1998: 172). This is not to say that facts and experience are unimportant. Rather, it is an acknowledgement of the possibility that rhetoric, symbols and fashion may sometimes win over substance in national policy-making.

First, if organisations are viewed as entities that should produce services rationally, efficiently and effectively, the ideas that are to guide organisational action must also be of a rationalistic character (Meyer 1996: 250). The self-regulation concept fitted this starting-point well, with its emphasis on 'bounded rationality' and localisation of decision-making at the level where the capacity to obtain detailed knowledge about the various aspects related to the decision was greatest.

Second, the self-regulation concept also fitted well with the notion that policy ideas must not only be rational, but they should also represent an improvement of current ideas of how to organise; in other words, they must be progressive (Abrahamson 1996: 117). To have a progressive profile was not a problem for the self-regulation concept, since this steering strategy represented a quite radical turn away from the governmental strategy of central planning and control that had dominated continental European higher education policy after 1945 (Van Vught 1989: 34).

Third, due to the general societal belief that there must be established organisational structures if certain ends are to be met, it is also important that policy ideas must propose more organisations and more organisational activities (Meyer 1996: 251). By advocating more autonomous institutions of higher education and, by that, supporting the emergence of a stronger and more developed institutional management of universities and colleges, the self-regulation concept also matched this requirement. The self-regulation steering strategy implied that higher education institutions should be mandated new tasks and new responsibilities – leading, in short, to 'more organisation'.

Fourth, if ideas that have all these characteristics are to be separated from other rational and progressive ideas on organising, they have to be fashionable (Abrahamson 1996: 117); that is, they have to relate to popular societal expectations (see also Barley & Kunda 1992; Hyczynski 1993; Clegg & Palmer 1996). The ideas must fit the specific policy context, or meta-policy (Majone 1989: 166). This term implies that policy ideas must be accepted by the intellectual super-structure that provides the political inputs, the ideas, theories and arguments that politics are made of. Abrahamsson's (1996: 259-260) ideas about a common market of rhetoric between various policy stakeholders (researchers, politicians, bureaucrats) could serve as an illustration of such an arena. Thus, it may be argued that the breakthrough of the self-regulation idea partly can be explained by the attention and support it had, not only in the political arena, but in higher education in general. Stensaker (1998) has shown that such a common market of rhetoric can be a strong force for advocating certain policy ideas. The emphasis the self-regulation strategy puts on institutional autonomy may in this respect have been an important element that in different camps was seen as attractive for building 'a cohesive organisation to sustain its intellectual advance' (Kells 1992: 38; see also Höltta 1995).

GOVERNMENTAL STEERING STRATEGIES REVISITED

The cybernetic foundations of the self-regulation concept are in line with the trans-scientific nature of many policy ideas. Majone (1989: 3) uses this term for arguing that the policy ideas launched during a policy-making process are seldom purely technical or purely political. Instead they are often stated in a 'scientific language' that provides some sort of scientific legitimacy. However, the policy problems addressed are in principle not answerable solely by science. The consequence is that policy ideas are open (and vulnerable) to a variety of political interpretations during the policy-making and policy-implementation process. Hence, it may be argued that the symbolic dimension of policy ideas is not only important for explaining the diffusion of the self-regulation concept with respect to higher education throughout Europe. It is also, in general, important for understanding how different and sometimes contradictory political interests can be represented in governmental reform intentions with respect to higher education. A look back on the reform initiatives taken, to change the state–higher education relationship in higher education in the late 1980s and the 1990s, gives an indication on how symbols and interests in various ways were mixed during the reform implementation.

Self-regulation as search for legitimacy

The spread of the self-regulation steering strategy did not in every country involved result in political actions through which authority and responsibilities were transferred from the central level to the higher education institutions. Neave and Van Vught (1991: 253) pointed already, in the early 1990s, to the tendency that the strategy of self-regulation was 'unveiled to the cacophony of governmental drums and bagpipes'. Instead of substantial reform aimed at the actual promotion of a self-regulating higher education system, many governments paid only lip service to the self-regulation ideas.

Normally the use of this governmental 'tool' is associated with the need to be accountable to the constituency (Vedung & Van der Doelen 1998: 126). Thus, one could interpret the lip service paid to the self-regulation concept, but lack of 'real' action, as typical for a state in search of public legitimacy (Weiler 1990; Neave 1998). Of importance here is the fact that the strategy of self-regulation was introduced in an era with fiscal restraints with respect to higher education, and more unstable national economies in general. Lundgren has argued that the important driving force behind governmental search for legitimacy

> concerns the relationships between national policy and the control of the national economy. With an increasing dependence on the international economy the possibilities to manage the national economy and the incentives for growth have decreased and changed in nature. This change has accentuated one basic problem for the modern state, to have a profound base for its legitimacy (…); a change in legitimisation in a situation of diminished economic control as the impetus for moving state reforms from cost-taking initiatives to symbolic reconstructions of existing institutions (Lundgren 1990: 26).

Thus, for many governments, symbolism and rhetoric are the only instruments that can be used when substantive politics are not possible or when they have failed (cf. Edelman 1977).

Self-regulation as political pragmatism

Parsons (1995: 369) has argued that the cybernetic perspective has had a considerable impact on organisational studies during the 1980s and 1990s. First, he claims that cybernetics, and the concept of self-regulation, has been central in theories about organisational learning, and the move towards emphasising cognition in organisational studies. Further, can cybernetics also be seen as one of the core ideas underlying the many managerial approaches that were introduced in the public sector at this time?

This suggests that, in many countries, policy initiatives towards increased self-regulation may have been blurred with other policy initiatives in higher education. It can, for example, be argued that the notion of the 'Evaluative State' (Neave 1988; 1998; Granheim et al. 1990), as well as the ideas forming the foundation for 'Managerialism' (Pollitt (1993) and 'New Public Management' (Lane 1997), relate in various ways to the self-regulation concept. While, for example, the development of evaluation systems relates well to the need for feedback mechanisms in a self-regulating system, managerialism and new public management have been linked with the ideas of greater institutional autonomy, and clearer specifications of roles and responsibilities in governmental steering in general.

The blurring of policies was often a result of governmental needs to 'pick and choose' between various steering concepts for being able to relate them to local problems and national characteristics. In many countries, policy implementation, for example, is claimed to be characterised by tradition, continuation and a particular policy-making culture 'in which an interactive and negotiative process is taking place over time, between those seeking to put policy into effect and those upon whom action depends' (Barrett & Fudge 1981: 25). The process of 'pick and choose' may consequently have provided some countries with a label as 'reluctant reformers' (Olsen & Peters 1994; Lægreid & Pedersen 1999; Lane 1997), or profiled them as countries that are able to 'transform' international policy ideas to a national context (Christensen & Lægreid 1998; 1999; Bleiklie et al 2000).

Such governmental pragmatism may still include a symbolic dimension, since adapting to international policy ideas may represent a double-edged sword. It provides the adopter with an image of being 'modern' and 'progressive'. However, the adopter might also experience problems when faced with the 'not invented here syndrome' (see also Dill 2001) that prevails in so many policy arenas. To 'pick and choose' between various concepts and ideas may in this situation be the right thing to do, and may provide the process with greater legitimacy.

Self-regulation as rational restructuring

Neave (1988) has argued that decentralising responsibility, a vital intention with the self-regulation strategy, created several advantages from a governmental point of view:

> first, debate is diffused away from the centre and forced to concentrate on the implications it holds for the individual university; second, by creating greater 'tactical latitude', a greater degree of initiative may be stimulated, with the result (hopefully) that the particular university will look to its own efforts rather than seek guidance and interpretation from central government; and third, such a system will give rise to the ability of individual universities – and thus, at an aggregate level, the whole higher education system – to undertake 'fine tuning' in response to local or regional circumstances, in response to changes in both the national and regional labour markets (Neave 1988: 13).

A decade later, Neave developed his arguments further by claiming that the rationale behind the governmental interests in the self-regulation strategy was not so much related to the centralisation-decentralisation dilemma as to the need to increase the adaptability of higher education in general.

> Self-regulation, which has sometimes been seen as an early step towards putting into place a 'cybernetic', self-adjusting, higher education system (...), can also be interpreted as the construction of an arrangement which sought to accelerate the pace at which higher education adjusted to external change (Neave 1998: 275).

As such, one may claim that it was 'change' rather than 'self-regulation' that was really on the political agenda in many European countries (see also Dill 2001).

This explanation highlights again the symbolic dimensions of the self-regulation concept. The blurring of various policy intentions into 'grander narratives' (the idea of self-regulation and increased institutional autonomy) also have the positive side-effect that the potential level of conflict decreases. According to Weiler, conflict is a fairly constant element in the pursuit of educational reforms in most countries, and tends to become

> particularly intense when it comes to plans of reform of the educational system in some major way. Since few such controversies can be solved by decree they will not simply disappear just because someone, no matter how authoritatively, says that they should (Weiler 1990: 52).

To carry out reforms based on attractive and convincing, but loosely coupled, policy ideas could in this situation be of vital importance for governments.

ON FUTURE CHANGE IN THE STATE–HIGHER EDUCATION RELATIONSHIP

A second look at the application of the self-regulation concept in the practice of higher education seems to indicate that the intended changes in the state-higher education relationship according to this governmental steering strategy were never realised in practise. As indicated by Maassen (2003), governmental steering has during the last decades taken on many forms, and, with respect to the delegation of authority, shifts have occurred vertically, horizontally and mixed vertically-horizontally. Vertical shifts can be observed where national responsibility is transferred to a supranational level within the EU, or from a national level to subnational or regional levels. Horizontal shifts have taken place from public to semi-public or private forms of authority, and mixed vertical-horizontal shifts can be observed in the rise of international semi-public or private accreditation agencies. Thus, the unidirectional (i.e. de-central) shift of governmental steering proposed by the self-regulation strategy seems far from realised.

However, our ambition with this chapter is not to point to 'failure' concerning the implementation of the self-regulation steering strategy, but to draw attention to the symbolic nature of this concept, and, more generally, the relevance of analysing the symbolic dimensions of popular policy ideas. The reason for this should be obvious. Even if self-regulation as a policy idea no longer dominates the higher education governance arena, current policy discussions concerning the role of concepts such as 'markets', 'performance', 'accountability' and 'entrepreneurialism', in higher education steering, could be informed and sharpened by having an open eye for the symbolic dimension of these concepts.

Not every change in the state-higher education relationship in Europe was necessarily a result of applying a self-regulation strategy. In the same way, future changes in the state-higher education relationship will not always be the result of an emerging higher education 'market', or a growing awareness of the actual 'performance' of higher education (see also Maassen 2003). In the same way, as we have done with the self-regulation concept, it is of interest to 'de-compose' many of the current buzzwords in higher education in terms of clarity and distinctiveness. Such a process would most likely disclose that these concepts also have a strong symbolic side that allows for a variety of interpretations.

In a time when traditional steering arrangements are destabilised, making it more difficult for governments to intervene in any given policy sector (Van Kersbergen & Van Waarden 2001), steering concepts with extensive symbolic value may become more important. In higher education such symbols are of particular importance, since direct 'steering' of the 'human factor' in academia is an impossible task (Maassen 1996). In this situation the advantage of symbols and language is that they exert great social power that can be used as a tool to change attitudes and provide new cognitive frames of action (Scott 1995: 129).

There is a long tradition in policy analysis to emphasise the 'hard' aspects of politics, such as formal decision-making and explicit political objectives. We would argue that there is a need to bring the 'softer' aspects of the political process to the forefront, where policy as a means to influence the public opinion and to create meaning is more emphasised.

As indicated by Meyer & Scott (1992: 256-257), some of the most effective policy-making in public education in the USA has not evolved from reforming organisational structures, but by normative and symbolic definitions of 'important' nation-wide problems. The self-regulation concept was also received quite positively in European higher education, despite warnings that this steering strategy in some countries actually could mean an abandoning of the governmental role as 'guardian angel' for the sector (Nybom 1993). The new cognitive frame created by the self-regulation concept in higher education may have influenced this process significantly.

Actually, one may even argue that it is the self-regulation concept that paved the way for the current policy buzzwords, such as 'market', 'performance' and 'entrepreneurialism' in higher education, suggesting that popular policy ideas such as self-regulation may have considerable impact even after they run out of fashion. The consequences this has for the current relationship between the state and higher education in Europe is that governmental steering strategies should be treated as cumulative and not as mutually exclusive (Maassen 2003). The latest European trend in the quality assurance of higher education, i.e. national accreditation systems, may serve as an illustration of the point. Accreditation is closely related to ideas of 'markets' and 'performance', and this form of quality assurance is in many countries introduced in addition to existing national quality assurance mechanisms more closely associated with the self-regulation concept. The result is an inflating number of steering arrangements in this policy area.

Peters (2001: 96) has criticised many current reform ideas and reform policies for representing 'an oversimplification of the complex dynamics of the public sector and the efforts to make it work better'. The neglecting of the symbolic dimension of policy ideas may be one of the major reasons for such oversimplification, and should, as we have argued in this chapter, be better understood and analysed if we are to be informed in a more effective way about the changes in the relationship between the state and higher education.

CONCLUSION

The rise of the self-regulation concept in European higher education came at a time when even the involved governments had to admit that the traditional centralised governmental steering approach did not lead to the intended outcomes. Allowing for the development of self-regulating higher education institutions and systems was expected to lead to a more effective, more efficient, more relevant, and better functioning of higher education institutions. It will be clear that these high expectations could not be met in practice, even in the countries where serious efforts were undertaken to actually implement a self-regulation strategy. Higher education systems are too complex, with too many different stakeholders involved, who represent different, sometimes competing interests. In short, the cultural and structural institutional infrastructure forming the multi-layered foundation under a higher education system, will not be changed dramatically in one direction, 'only' as a consequence of a change in governmental steering strategy (Maassen 1996).

Nonetheless, the concept of self-regulation has remained relevant and attractive since its introduction in the 1980s for many actors involved in the debates on higher education steering, even though it has been marginalised somewhat in the larger public sector reforms of the 1990s. Especially the actors representing the sector itself still embrace the notion of a self-regulating higher education system. One could argue that from the perspective of the field of higher education, self-regulation comes close to being the 'ideal' steering strategy, based on a high level of trust between the actors involved. However, from the side of the government, self-regulation has gradually become identified with 'lack of control'. Despite the obvious advantages of a higher education sector that is taking care of its own affairs without too much direct government interference, the everyday political practice in every country sooner or later seems to emphasise the notion of control more than the notion of trust. However, not only the government should be 'blamed' in this. It can be argued that in the evolving self-regulating systems each higher education institution was mainly 'regulating its own interests', thereby neglecting the interests of the higher education system as a whole, as well as the general public interest in higher education. This is certainly one of the reasons why new steering concepts were introduced that allowed the government to develop system level control mechanisms, such as bilateral 'performance contracts' with each institution. However, the introduction of new steering instruments did not mean that the self-regulatory instruments were abolished. A core example in this can be found in the area of quality assessment. As part of the implementation of the self-regulation steering strategy, the responsibility for guaranteeing the quality of higher education was no longer in the hands of the government. New bodies were established either with an independent status or owned by the institutions. Most of these bodies still exist, but, in addition, all kinds of parallel quality assessment measures have been taken under the instigation of the government. These new measures were not always linked to the self-regulatory quality assessment bodies. Also, other examples can be given of situations where self-regulation instruments are functioning parallel to or integrated with new steering instruments. These can all be regarded as forms of institutional change in higher education whereby a new institutional layer is 'deposited' on top of the previous one (Tolbert & Zucker 1996). This sedimentation of policy ideas in higher education can be expected to lead to even more complex and even contradictory steering arrangements, and indicate that, even if policy ideas apparently run out of fashion, they may still have a considerable impact on the relationship between the state and higher education in the years to come.

REFERENCES

Abrahamsson, E. (1996). Technical and Aesthetic Fashion. In Czarniavska, B. & Sevon, G. (eds.), *Translating Organizational Change*. Berlin: Walter de Greuyter.

Aamodt, P. O., Kyvik, S. & Skoie, H. Norway: Towards a More Indirect Model of Governance? In: Neave, G. and Van Vught, F. A. (1991). *Prometheus Bound. The Changing Relationship Between Government and Higher Education*. Oxford: Pergamon Press.

Barley, S. R. & Kunda, G. (1992). Design and Devotion: Surges of Rational and Normative Ideologies of Control in Management Discourse. *Administrative Science Quarterly*, 37(3), 363-399.

Barrett, S. & Fudge, C. (eds.) (1981), *Policy and Action*. London: Methuen.

Birnbaum, R. (1989). *How Colleges Work: the Cybernetics of Academic Organization and Leadership*. San Francisco: Jossey-Bass.

Bleiklie, I., Høstaker, R. & Vabø, A. (2000). *Policy and Practice in Higher Education. Reforming Norwegian Universities*. London: Jessica Kingsley Publishers.

Clegg, S. R. & Palmer, G. (eds.) (1996). *The Politics of Management Knowledge*. London: Sage Publications.

Christensen, T. & Lægreid, P. (1998). *Transforming New Public Management. A study of how modern reforms are received in the Norwegian civil service*. Bergen: LOS-senteret.

Christensen, T. & Lægreid, P. (1999). New Public Management – the trade-off between political governance and administrative autonomy. Paper presented at the *Third international research Symposium on Public management*, Aston University, Birmingham, 25-26 March.

Dill, D. D. (2001). The Regulation of Public Research Universities: Changes in academic competition and implications for university autonomy and accountability. *Higher Education Policy*, 14, 21-35.

Edelman, M. (1977). *Political language. Words That succeed and Politics That Fail*. London: Academic Press.

Granheim, M., Kogan, M. & Lundgren, U. (1990). *Evaluation as policymaking*. London: Jessica Kingsley Publishers.

Henkel, M. (2000). *Academic Identities and Policy Change in Higher Education*. London: Jessica Kingsley Publishers.

Hood, C. (1998). *The Art of the State. Culture, Rhetoric and Public Management*. Oxford: Clarendon Press.

Hyczynski, A. A. (1993). Explaining the Succession of Management Fads. *International Journal of Human Resource Management*, 4(2), 443-463.

Hölttä, S. (1995). *Towards the Self-regulative University*. Publications from the Social Sciences No. 23. Joensuu: University of Joensuu.

Kells, H. (1992). *Self-regulation in Higher Education. A Multi-national perspective on collaborative systems of quality assurance and control*. London: Jessica Kingsley Publishers.

Lane, J-E. (1997). *Public Sector Reform. Rationale, Trends and Problems*. London: Sage publications.

Lægreid, P. (1999). *Administrative reforms in Scandinavia – testing the co-operative model*. Bergen: LOS-senteret.

Lægreid, P. & Pedersen, O.K. (1999). *Fra opbygning til ombygning i staten : organisationsforandringer i tre nordiske lande*, København: Jurist og økonomforbundets forlag.

Lundgren, U. (1990). Educational Policymaking, Decentralisation and Evaluation. In Granheim, M., Kogan, M. & Lundgren, U. *Evaluation as policymaking*. London: Jessica Kingsley Publishers.

Maassen, P. (1996). *Governmental steering and the academic culture. The intangibility of the human factor in Dutch and German universities*. Utrecht: De Tijdstroom.

Maassen, P. A. M. (2003). Shifts in Governance Arrangements. An interpretation of the introduction of new management structures in higher education. In: Amaral, A., I.M. Larsen, and L. Meek (eds.), *The Higher Education Managerial Revolution*. Dordrecht: Kluwer Academic Publishers. (Forthcoming).

Maassen, P. & Van Vught, F.A. (1989). *Dutch higher education in transition*. Culemborg: LEMMA.

Maassen, P. & Van Vught, F.A. (1996). *Inside Academia*. Utrecht: LEMMA.

Majone, G. (1989). *Evidence, Argument and the Persuasion in the Policy process*. London: Yale University Press.

Meyer, J. W. (1996). Otherhood. The promulgation and transmission of ideas in the modern organizational environment. In Czarniavska, B. & Sevon, G. (eds.) *Translating Organizational Change*. Berlin: Walter de Greuyter.

Meyer, J. W. & Scott, W.R. (1992). *Organizational environments. Ritual and Rationality*. London: Sage Publications.

Neave, G. (1988). On the Cultivation of Quality, Efficiency and Enterprise: An overview of recent trends in higher education in Western Europe. *European Journal of Education*, 23(1), 7- 23.

Neave, G. (1988). The Evaluative State Re-Considered. *European Journal of Education*, 33(3), 265-284.

Neave, G. & Van Vught, F.A. (1991). *Prometheus Bound. The Changing Relationship Between Government and Higher Education*. Oxford: Pergamon Press.

Nybom, T. (1993). The Constitutional determintants and Future of Qualified Knowledge Production. Paper presented to the *Working Conference on International and Comparative Higher Education*, Penn State University, 1-2 November.

Olsen, J. P. & Peters, B.G. (1994). *Lessons from Experience. Experimental Learning in administrative Rfeorms in Eight Democracies*. Oslo: ARENA, working paper no. 3.

Parsons, W. (1995). *Public Policy. An introduction to the theory and practise of policy analysis*. Aldershot: Edward Elgar.

Peters, B.G. (2001). *The Future of Governing (Second Edition, revised)*. Lawrence, KS: University Press of Kansas.

Pollitt, C. (1993). *Managerialism and the Public Services. Cuts or Cultural Changes in the 1990s?* Oxford: Blackwell Publishers.

Reed, M., Meek, L. V. & Jones, G. (2002). Introduction. In Amaral, A., Jones, G. and B. Karseth (eds.) *Governing Higher Education: National perspectives on institutional governance*. Dordrecht: Kluwer Academic Publishers.

Stensaker, B. (1998). Culture and fashion in reform implementation: perceptions and adaptations of management reforms in higher education. *Journal of Higher Education Policy and Management*, 20(2): 129-138.

Tolbert, P.S. & Zucker, L.G. (1996). The Institutionalization of Institutional Theory. In: Clegg, S., C. Hardy, and W.R. Nord (eds.) *Handbook of Organization Studies*. Thousand Oaks, Ca: Sage.

Van Vught, F.A. (ed.) (1989). *Governmental Strategies and Innovation in Higher Education*. London: Jessica Kingsley Publishers.

Van Kersbergen, K. & Van Waarden, F. (2001). Shifts in Governance: Problems of Legitimacy and Accountability. Paper on the theme 'Shifts in Governance' as part of the *Strategic Plan 2002-2005 of the Netherlands Organization for Scientific Research*.

Vedung, E. & Van der Doelen, F,C.J. (1998). The Sermon: Information programs in the Public policy Process – Choice, Effects and Evaluation. In: Bemelmans-Videc, M-L., Rist, R. & Vedung, E., *Carrots, Sticks and Sermons. Policy instruments and Their Evaluation*. London: Transaction Publishers.

Weiler, H. (1990). Decentralisation in Educational Givernance: An exercise in contradiction? In: Granheim, M., Kogan, M. & Lundgren, U. *Evaluation as policymaking*. London: Jessica Kingsley Publishers.

BARBARA SPORN

MANAGEMENT IN HIGHER EDUCATION:

CURRENT TRENDS AND FUTURE PERSPECTIVES IN EUROPEAN COLLEGES AND UNIVERSITIES

Abstract. The management of higher education has been challenged during recent decades. Especially in Europe, increased institutional autonomy and accountability initiated changes in methods and tools of management. These range from management by objectives and contracts, entrepreneurial approaches, steering from a distance, to service and customer orientation. This chapter will discuss trends in European higher education systems which have led to new approaches in university management. Firstly, globalisation and internationalisation created a more competitive environment. Secondly, harmonisation of degrees and study programmes increased comparability among European systems. Thirdly, marketisation has triggered calls for the entrepreneurial university. Fourthly, the role of the state has profoundly changed based on a more public management approach. All these trends can be translated into management implications. They involve new governance and leadership structures as well as new management techniques. The chapter will conclude by introducing models of university management which have appeared in many of the EAIR discourses: the entrepreneurial, the adaptive, and the learning university.

INTRODUCTION

Colleges and universities in Europe have experienced a period of change and transformation since the early 1990s. Both in continental Europe and in the UK, the role of the state has been shifting with the general goal to make systems of higher education more efficient and effective. Thereby, general participation rates of the age cohort should rise and institutions of higher education should be steered based on a corporate rather than a collegial model. With this development, the management of higher education has become increasingly important.

Management here means the structures and processes of leadership, governance and administration. When thinking about management, it is important to keep the idiosyncratic nature of higher education institutions in mind (Baldridge, Curtis, Ecker & Riley 1977; Clark 1983; Weick 1976). Colleges and universities are known for their ambiguous goals, multiple constituencies, unclear technologies, the role of professionalism (or professors) and environmental vulnerability. Models describing this specific nature range from organised anarchy (Cohen & March 1974), loosely coupled systems (Weick 1976), collegial, bureaucratic, and political approaches (Birnbaum 1989), to adhocracy (Mintzberg 1979). Management has to take this into account and develop a corresponding approach or style. Often, questions of shared governance, the role of leadership and the shift from bureaucratic compliance to professional management are of major concern.

For EAIR, the management drive has also started in the 1990s. More and more contributions to the discourse of institutional researchers, scholars, policy makers and administrators revolved around instruments, approaches, strength and weakness as well as models for improving the performance of colleges and universities through

97

R. Begg (ed.), The Dialogue between Higher Education Research and Practice, 97–107.
© 2003 *Kluwer Academic Publishers. Printed in the Netherlands.*

professional management. With the rise of new public management and the changing role of the state the management function has gained prominence.

Burton Clark, the renowned higher education expert, once distinguished between the top (i.e. state-level policies), the middle (i.e. institutional leadership), and the bottom (i.e. academic units and faculty) level and described national systems of higher education accordingly (1983). Based on that, European higher education policies can be described as strengthening the middle level thereby emphasising institutional management and leadership. In this chapter, special attention is paid to trends and developments in Europe which have led to those large-scale institutional changes. Issues such as globalisation, harmonisation, marketisation and new public management will be discussed. Following that, this chapter will analyse new ways of governance, management and leadership within colleges and universities. The last part will focus on three ideas which have been presented at EAIR Forum meetings over the years representing the current discussion in higher education management.

DEVELOPMENTS IN EUROPE

Europe has seen some major changes of its higher education systems within the last several years if not decades. Those issues relevant for higher education management encompass globalisation and internationalisation, harmonisation of systems, marketisation and managerialism, and new public management.

Globalisation has triggered many systems in Europe to adopt a more US or Anglo-Saxon system of higher education. The goal of state policies has been to widen access for a larger group of the age cohort and to expand and diversify the respective system of higher education. As a consequence, many countries introduced vocational colleges and private universities. Also, virtual institutions and branch campuses of international universities proliferated in Continental Europe. To speak with a 'classic' distinction coined by Martin Trow, Europe seems to move from elite, to mass, to universal higher education (Trow 1973). Of course, the tradition of public higher education in most European countries has been put under pressure with those new developments and plans. Examples range from Austria and Switzerland introducing Fachhochschulen (i.e. vocational colleges), Scandinavia and the Netherlands permitting private universities, and France and Spain developing a quality assurance mechanism thereby establishing new types of institutions.

Internationalisation in Europe has been aiming to create a European space of higher education. Under the word 'Bologna' some major changes have been happening mainly concerning the teaching function of higher education. A new area of learning is planned to develop which would make it easier for students and scholars to move freely. In general, the Bologna declaration of 1999 signed by 29 countries promotes the following themes: comparable degrees, two main cycles of studies (bachelor and master), a credit transfer system, mobility for students and staff, cooperation in quality assurance, and the development of a European dimension in higher education1. This way, European systems of higher education would become more homogeneous. At the same time, competitive pressure would increase both within Europe and with other parts of the world – mainly the US. Mobility of students and staff would internationalise institutions and place emphasis on providing the necessary resources.

For many institutions, Bologna means restructuring the curriculum and helping students to move through scholarships. Management implications range from having top leadership positions dealing with internationalisation within colleges and universities to service units which advise and organise international opportunities for students and staff.

The marketisation of higher education has been a consequence of the withdrawal of the state from its control function. In many countries of Europe, the state control has been replaced by a market approach to steering institutions of higher education. Marketisation is probably the most severe change in European higher education. As noted earlier, a diversification of the higher education market and the increased mobility of students and staff can be observed. This implies competition among institutions for resources and all kinds of different target groups. On the institutional level, marketisation means privatisation in the sense of pushing universities into more private industry mechanisms like financial control, accounting, and a cost or even profit centre philosophy. Professors and staff are becoming more entrepreneurial. Financial income is more diverse with tuition being one source. Longer-term budgets which are performance based create the need to establish financial management techniques. Institutions are becoming more autonomous to manage their own 'business'. One major reason for this change is the increased pressure on fiscal budgets and the need to make systems more efficient and effective. Many countries experience high drop-out rates and long time to degrees. With a more competitive and market-like behaviour, the role of the client gains importance and universities start to think about service-orientation.

Still, while marketisation plays an important role also as a metaphor for what policy makers desire, it needs to be kept in mind that legal regulations are still in place. Very often, the overall system is regulated by laws and regulations directly from ministries and government offices. Sometimes even contradicting rules can be implemented which might have adverse effects on the system. For example, in Austria, the government sticks to its open access policy for universities but permits vocational colleges to select their students. As a consequence, students with less qualifications tend to end up as university students. Hence, it is important when looking at European higher education to understand that, even though the state withdrew from its traditional role, there is still enough interest to regulate the market for higher education by setting up the rules of competition.

Many researchers have paid attention to this new and very prominent trend towards marketisation in Europe (Askling, Bauer & Marton 1999; Bauer, Askling, Gerard-Marton & Marton 1999; Clark 1998; Kieser 2000; Kogan, Bauer, Bleiklie & Henkel 2000). Their major concern has been the shift from the academic, collegial model to institutional managerialism. No longer do the professionals of the institution (i.e. professors) have the final decision and power over institutional matters. A new form of management seems to be on the rise which involves professional managers using instruments and techniques from business enterprises. Conflict and contestation can often be the consequence. There are warnings that colleges and universities might lose their identity as social institutions and change to a knowledge industry model. (Gumport & Pusser 1997; Gumport 2000; Slaughter & Leslie 1997)

The cause and basis for these trends in Europe is new public management. As most European nations dominantly have public systems of higher education, the rise of neo-liberal politics and policies lead to a new view on colleges and universities. The major underlying reason is financial. Through tight state budgets and fiscal crises, the state needs to cut funding for higher education.

In general new public management includes trends towards privatisation, increased managerialism and marketisation, attempts to establish quasi-markets, the rise of cost-consciousness (i.e. providing 'value for money' or doing 'more with less', the use of performance indicators, auditing systems and central monitoring, and the management of change by high-profile chief executive officers in charge of public institutions (Ferlie, Ashburner, Fitzgerald & Pettigrew 1996). New public management applied to higher education took yet a different pathway. For example, in Sweden, state policy makers used the total quality movement to restructure higher education (Bauer & Henkel 1997; Stensaker 2000). In Norway, new public management called for efficiency measures, decentralization of authority to the institutions, and performance targets to enhance higher education institutions (Bleiklie, Hostaker & Vabo 2000). In the UK, the quality movement has been especially prominent as a way of new public management. Evidence are the numerous centres, programmes, publications and journals, and individual faculty members specializing in this area. Through clear indicators and resource allocation based on performance, academic cultures and managerial values have changed dramatically (Kogan & Hanney 2000). Still, research shows that those reforms have only been implemented superficially and the intended shift in values has not happened (Henkel 2000).

As this part of the chapter has demonstrated, large changes have been occurring in Europe over the last decade. Especially the management function will be of greater and critical importance when it comes to establishing modern, more competitive institutions. Now we will turn to the specific management issues which have been emerging over the last 25 years both within EAIR and outside.

MANAGEMENT ISSUES

The management of higher education involves three distinct features: governance, leadership and management. Governance refers to the structure and processes of decision-making. Leadership implies the role of top-level positions taking responsibility for the overall institution. Management refers to the operational side of running an institution, i.e. the structures and processes by which decisions are planned, implemented and controlled (Sporn 1999).

Within the last twenty-five years higher education has experienced some major changes in institutional management. This has mainly been caused by introducing a new model for the relationship between the institutions and the state (Gornitzka 1999). This new steering approach meant moving away from a state-control to a state-supervising model. Thereby the position of the government vis-à-vis colleges and universities has been 'at a distance'. New views of governance, management and leadership emerged, which were based more on a new public management tradition.

The roots of those changes can be found in the historic development of European higher education. In the 1960s and 1970s democratic, internally-oriented governance and leadership structures were in place. Those proved to be inefficient and ineffective as they evolved into overloaded and under-prepared decision-making bodies which took too long time periods for their decision. They were also incapable of reacting fast and innovatively to change in the environment. Hence, in the late 1980s and early 1990s, state ministries of higher education introduced an externally oriented, more managerial approach. A push towards leaner organisations and a power structure which emphasised individuals over collectives developed. The goal has been to represent stakeholder interests inside the institution and to grant as much autonomy as possible.

One major change has been the governance of colleges and universities. Again, it is important to note that governments and state ministries use governance structures to redefine steering of its higher education organisations. Going back to the work of Burton Clark (1983), the traditional continental European model had the state and the academics as the major players in governance issues with little influence of the middle, institutional leadership level. With the rise of neo-liberal policies, a dramatic shift towards institutional autonomy empowered central administration and leadership (i.e. rectors and presidents of institutions, deans and heads of institutes or departments). Also, new stakeholders (as board members) were introduced, which would represent general societal interests and work for the overall benefit of the institution (Maassen 2000).

New governance structures in Europe meant a redefined role for the rector, the senate, the faculty, the administration and external stakeholders. In general, the power of the senate has been reduced to issues closer to their core responsibilities, i.e. teaching and research. It lost its importance because it had proven to be too large and inflexible to provide the necessary innovation for the institution. In many cases, such as the Netherlands, the senate has even moved to an advisory role (De Boer, 2001). At the same time, new structures evolved which combined a collegial with a leadership function: a board of trustees, an executive board and a faculty board. Leaders (i.e. rectors, deans, etc.) often head those boards and are responsible and accountable for implementing decisions accordingly.

A relatively new stakeholder model in higher education governance led to the introduction of a board of trustees model in Europe. Board members represent very important stakeholders of the individual institution who can range from business managers, politicians, professors or international experts. The board in most cases elects the rector and his or her team, approves all strategic documents (e.g. organisational structure, budgets, strategy), and can vote against any malpractice of top managers at the institution. The board members tend to come from outside the institution and are mostly accountable to the ministry. Appointments to such boards are a contested issue and can range from purely ministerial to a combination of institutional and governmental nominations. Boards in that sense have an important external control and linkage function with the ministry and society at large.

The second form of collegial governance structures are executive boards. In many European countries these consist of the rector and a team of vice-rectors. They make decisions at the top-level of the institution and all are appointed by the board of trustees. This has also meant a major change, as in the past they were elected by the academic community. There often is a functional divide with responsibilities ranging from research to international affairs and board members decide upon resource allocation, promotion procedures, and general infrastructure.

The third form which is mostly used by comprehensive, multi-faculty institutions is a faculty board. At this level, major areas for decision-making concern the core function of universities in teaching and research. Hence, this board would usually consist of the respective dean and other members of the faculty. They recommend new and evaluate old study programmes and decide at the first level on promotion and tenure. Often, a programme committee can be found which helps preparing the decision-making.

As can be easily understood this new governance structure has provoked a substantial debate and even conflict. Only through some guiding principles could more damage be avoided. First, double or twofold legitimisation has been a way to unite top-down and bottom-up approaches at all levels (Müller-Böling 1998). The general idea has been to have one level suggesting and another level choosing a person to serve on a governing board or in a leadership role. The intention has been to have the unit or group affected the most making a binding suggestion and to give choice to the level of leadership having to implement major changes.

The leadership of colleges and universities has been strengthened over the years of reform of European higher education. The rector and/or president have been established as the key figures and major players steering the institution. The traditional role has been the one of a primus inter pares, i.e. a person elected by the university community with the main task to represent the institution in academic and ceremonial matters. This view has changed dramatically. The rector is coming to be an appointed leader by the board. The role can be compared to that of a CEO or head of the board of directors. Responsibilities encompass the planning and implementing of all major areas ranging from budget and space to teaching and research. He or she is accountable for the success or failure of the institution. In some countries like Austria, the rector is the one signing performance contracts with the ministry thereby negotiating major indicators and measures.

The rector's role is moving from representative to professional. This implies that the rector no longer automatically comes from the faculty of the institution involved. Large searches are instituted to find candidates with the necessary qualification. Certainly, some academic credentials are obligatory (as the US example shows well, with presidents and deans normally having a faculty background) but an equivalent expertise like management of a research institute could be an adequate substitute. A career track has been developing in Europe which calls for a new way to prepare candidates for the job. Some centres, institutes and universities already provide programmes and it can be expected that their number will increase. With this comes the need for new salary schemes which are more competitive. Only with these factors in place, can a good and qualitative set of experts be attracted. Overall, professional leadership with an academic background and a full-time position will be the future at many colleges and universities.

Leadership structures have to combine responsibility and accountability. In many European countries, the practice has been to divide strategic and operational levels of decision-making and leadership. The consequence has been that committees decided (sometimes without the necessary background information, data or preparation) on issues for which they then have not been held accountable. One such example could be senates deciding upon a budget plan, where a realistic picture could never evolve but individual interests are dominated by academic unit needs. The new direction points to reuniting responsibility and accountability, e.g. a senate deciding upon issues of teaching and research (tenure, academic programmes) and rectors negotiating a budget with the board and ministry.

Still at the leadership level, a new set of positions is emerging. Vice-Rectors, deans, or programme directors have taken over certain areas. These can range from finance, research and teaching, and international relations to undergraduate and graduate programmes. Again, responsibility and accountability should be combined to guarantee quality outcomes. Candidates are often found within the faculty of the institution, often on a full-time basis with special financial incentives. They can be an important liaison between the faculty and the administration. Trust and identification seem to be one of the most important success factors in today's colleges and universities. From European universities it can be learnt that a faculty-dominated administration and top-level leadership group can help the institution to thrive and overcome major obstacles (Rhoades & Sporn 2002; Sporn 1995). Paying close attention to integrating academic personnel with managerial personnel needs to be kept in mind (Clark 1997).

The management of colleges and universities is defined as the structures and processes by which decisions are implemented. In a sense, structures imply the role of administration and processes mean instruments and tools of management. Looking back the last twenty-five years reveals that a tremendous change occurred within colleges and universities. In the 1970s, European universities and colleges were based on a bureaucratic model of management with a divided organisational structure, i.e. a state bureaucracy at individual institutions responsible for compliance to legal requirements and a academic guild providing the core services in teaching and research. Following this period, a collegial form of management evolved. This type can be characterised as institutional management and administration firmly rooted in the faculty. Professors have taken over major administrative positions that involve 'running the institution'. With the rise of a new policy in higher education, more market pressure and the call for professionalism, a managerial approach to administration developed. This meant the use and adoption of private industry tools such as performance indicators, personnel development and standard reporting. Most recently, entrepreneurial forms of management have appeared. Here institutional leadership sets up certain incentive structures for individual members of the faculty to create opportunities for raising funds and generally doing business. Accountability and responsibility for most activities are decentralised to the person in charge. The top-level management solely provides an infrastructure and controls for results (Sporn 1999).

In European systems of higher education a mix of these models (i.e. bureaucratic, collegial, managerial, entrepreneurial) are present. Still, there are a couple of 'principles' which have been dominating the discussions about university management over the last years both at EAIR Forums and within institutions. Those include: management by objectives and contracts, performance indicators, ex-post steering, and professionalisation.

Contract management and management by objectives is one of the leading principles in European higher education. Those are tightly connected to the notion of performance measurement and funding, and have been developed due to the new role of the state and the rise of new public management. As universities and colleges in Europe will still be funded mostly out of state budgets, there is a need for quality control and accountability. Hence, contracts were created as a tool both between the ministries and universities and inside the institutions. Those contracts normally consist of a fixed sum and a flexible budget element which is based on reaching performance targets and objectives. Performance is measured by certain indicators and can range from research productivity and entering students to graduates.

Ex-post and ex-ante steering is a principle related to contract management. Universities can be funded for the input they can process or they can be evaluated based on their output. Some authors and policy makers have called for a strong move from input to output views of management in steering colleges and universities (Müller-Böling 1998).

One other important principle in current university management is professionalisation. This topic has been on the agenda of many meetings, EAIR Fora, educational programmes, and discussions of university administrators. Professionalisation often means moving from personnel being trained as state bureaucrats, to managers with a relevant degree. Rectors, presidents, directors, deans and the like often come to the job ill-prepared and with wrong assumptions. For a university to manage its own enterprise without the help of the ministry more professionalism is needed. This would include knowledge in leadership, personnel development programmes, financial control and marketing. As some examples in the UK and the Netherlands demonstrate, a new market for university managers will evolve. Academic programmes are being offered and managers from related industries get interested and mobile enough to be accept a university management position. Competitive salaries and international searches will be the next step. The biggest challenge is to understand and be prepared for the idiosyncratic nature of institutions of higher education. A blind adoption of business practices is doomed to fail (Birnbaum 2000) and will not work.

After this short description of current issues in management of higher education some future perspectives of higher education management will conclude this chapter. As the argument has been that universities and colleges are under pressure from the external environment and are facing a demand-response imbalance, this last part of the chapter will introduce three models prominent in the literature to manage this situation: the learning university, the entrepreneurial university and the adaptive university.

FUTURE PERSPECTIVES

There are different themes which have been coined by higher education researchers to describe trends about where colleges and universities, especially in Europe, might move. Of course this list is not exhaustive but rather represents a choice of some of the most prominent and important concepts which institutions of higher education have developed over recent decades.

The notion of the learning university is interesting as it resonates both with the core function of universities, i.e. teaching and research, and with the concepts of organisational learning applied to institutions of higher education (Askling & Kristensen 1999; Dill 1999). Main promoters of this idea have been members of the EAIR community for many years. The underlying thoughts about the learning university are twofold. On the one hand, the university must provide an atmosphere where student learning can be enhanced to an optimum. This would include having a teacher training unit and modern technology available in the classroom. The relationship between teacher and student is redefined and a learning sphere develops which supports aspirations, reflexion, discussion, and the understanding of complexity. On the other hand, universities as learning organisations have to restructure in order to react flexibly and proactively to a dynamically changing environment. Authors have promoted a couple of factors which should be taken into consideration (Senge 2000): the role of line managers, academic units as change agents, university leaders learning from private industry, self-organised restructuring, driving forces of change through faculty involvement, and internal networks. Yet another series of factors focuses on organisational architecture to enhance university learning (Dill 1999): systematic problem solving, learning from own experience, learning from others, and experimentation with new approaches, transferring knowledge, and measuring learning. Overall, the learning approach enables university leaders and policy makers to take a fresh look at the structures and processes of innovation at colleges and universities.

The idea of an adaptive university is based on the assumption that institutional management needs to understand and consider its external environment in order to survive and thrive. In this sense, university administration and management can either buffer or bridge any threats or opportunities in 'the market' or industry (Pfeffer & Salancik 1978). Choices can range from choosing to work in a new environment, to changing university structures. Structures and processes of adaptation involve a leadership which is committed and has a supportive role, i.e. providing resources for initiatives and projects triggered by the core units. Management should be professional and shared governance involving both faculty and administration should be in place. Differentiation of structure is an important prerequisite of adaptation. In order to respond flexibly, a differentiated set of basic organisational units can help to respond to a diverse set of external demands. Clear goals will then provide sufficient direction for all university activities. An entrepreneurial culture can set the grounds for a climate where individual projects get rewarded and institutional interests (and finances) are protected (Sporn 1999).

The entrepreneurial university is a phenomenon which has been widely discussed in Europe. Case studies of European universities lead to the conclusion that, in some cases, universities can be turned into entrepreneurial enterprises. This transformation is based on five crucial factors (Clark 1998): a strengthened steering core, an expanded developmental periphery, a diversified funding base, a stimulated academic heartland, and an integrated entrepreneurial culture. With a more autonomous status, universities in Europe will be in the position to steer independently through a strengthened core thereby embracing central managerial groups and academic departments. Through an entrepreneurial periphery, linkages with outside organisations and groups at the border of the institution can help to reach across traditional boundaries. Differentiated funding, including public monies but also corporate and private giving, can enhance the independence of the institution and increase flexibility. The academic units (as the heartland of every university) need to be integrated and respected for their central role as the sole providers of teaching and research. New belief systems in the universities need to be worked out between managerial groups and the academics. A culture which supports change will form the basis of the entrepreneurial university. It can start out as a small idea and turn into a firm set of beliefs about where the institution is going. It is important that the institutional perspective goes beyond individual interests and tries to move and transform the whole university.

In summary, this chapter has shown how changes in the external environment of universities have lead to new management practices at colleges and universities in Europe. Different approaches have been introduced to show the current status of European higher education. With three models mostly discussed in policy, scholarly, and management arenas, different outlooks for the future have been provided. EAIR is a Forum where the exchange and questioning of any one of those ideas will continuously occur. It remains to be seen what new approaches will be found and implemented. EAIR will be there to learn from each other so that the wheel of European university management needs not to be reinvented over again.

NOTE

1 http://europa.eu.int/comm/education/socrates/erasmus/bologna.pdf

REFERENCES

Askling, B., Bauer, M. & Marton, S. (1999). Swedish Universities towards Self-Regulation: A New Look at Institutional Autonomy. *Tertiary Education And Management, 5*(2), 175-195.

Askling, B. & Kristensen, B. (1999, August 22-25, 1999). Towards *"The Learning University"*: *Implications for institutional governance and academic autonomy*. Paper presented at the EAIR Forum 1999, Lund, Sweden.

Baldridge, J. V., Curtis, D. V., Ecker, G. P. & Riley, G. L. (1977). Alternative Models of Governance in Higher Education. In G. L. Riley & J. V. Baldridge (eds.), *Governing Academic Organization*s (pp. 2-25). Berkeley, CA: McCutchan.

Bauer, M., Askling, B., Gerard-Marton, S. & Marton, F. (1999). *Transforming Universities: Changing Patterns of Governance, Structure and Learning in Swedish Higher Education*. London: Jessica Kingsley.

Bauer, M. & Henkel, M. (1997). Responses of academe to quality reforms in higher education: a comparative study of England and Sweden. *Tertiary Education and Management, 3*(3), 211-228.

Birnbaum, R. (1989). *How Colleges Work: The Cybernetics of Academic Organization and Leadership*. San Francisco: Jossey-Bass.

Birnbaum, R. (2000). *Management Fads in Higher Education: Where They Come From, What They Do, Why They Fail*. Chichester: John Wiley.

Bleiklie, I., Hostaker, R. & Vabo, A. (2000). *Policy and Practice in Higher Education: Reforming Norwegian Universities*. London: Jessica Kingsley.

Clark, B. R. (1983). *The Higher Education System: Academic Organization in Cross-National Perspective*. Berkeley, CA: University of California Press.

Clark, B. R. (1997). *Small worlds, different worlds: The uniqueness and troubles of American academic professions*. Daedalus, 126(4), 21-42.

Clark, B. R. (1998). *Creating Entrepreneurial Universities: Organizational Pathways of Transformation*. Oxford: Pergamon.

Cohen, M. D. & March, J. G. (1974). *Leadership and Ambiguity: The American College President* (Second ed.). Boston: Harvard Business School Press.

De Boer, H. (2001). On Limitations and Consequences of Change: Dutch University Governance in Transition. *Tertiary Education and Management, 7*(2), 163-180.

Dill, D. D. (1999). Academic Accountability and University Adaptation: The Architecture of an Academic Learning Organization. *Higher Education*, 38, 127-154.

Ferlie, E., Ashburner, L., Fitzgerald, L. & Pettigrew, A. (1996). *The New Public Management in Action*. Oxford: Oxford University Press.

Gornitzka, Å. (1999). Governmental policies and organisational change in higher education. *Higher Education*, 38(1), 5-31.

Gumport, P. & Pusser, B. (1997). Restructuring the Academic Environment. In M. W. Peterson & D. D. Dill & L. A. Mets (eds.), *Planning and Management for a Changing Environment: A Handbook on Redesigning Postsecondary Institutions* (pp. 453-478). San Francisco: Jossey-Bass.

Gumport, P. J. (2000). Academic restructuring: Organizational change and institutional imperatives. *Higher Education*, 39(1), 67-91.

Henkel, M. (2000). *Academic Identities and Policy Change in Higher Education*. London: Jessica Kingsley.

Kieser, A. (2000). Alternative Organisationsmodelle autonomer Universitäten. In S. Titscher & G. Winckler & H. Biedermann & H. Gatterbauer & S. Laske & R. Moser & F. Strehl & F. Wojda & H. Wulz (eds.), *Universitäten im Wettbewerb - Zur Neustrukturierung österreichischer Universitäten* (pp. 234-282). München: Rainer Hampp.

Kogan, M., Bauer, M., Bleiklie, I. & Henkel, M. (2000). *Transforming Higher Education - A Comparative Study*. London: Jessica Kingsley.

Kogan, M. & Hanney, S. (2000). *Reforming Higher Education*. London: Jessica Kingsley.

Maassen, P. (2000). The Changing Roles of Stakeholders in Dutch University Governance. *European Journal of Education*, 35(4), 449-464.

Mintzberg, H. (1979). *The Structuring of Organizations*. Englewood Cliffs, NJ: Prentice-Hall.

Müller-Böling, D. (1998). University Governance as Conflictual Management. In D. Müller-Böling & E. Mayer & A. J. MacLachlan & J. Fedrowitz (eds.), *University in Transition. Research Mission - Interdisciplinarity - Governance* (pp. 231-245). Gütersloh: Bertelsmann Foundation.

Pfeffer, J. & Salancik, G. R. (1978). *The External Control of Organizations - A Resource Dependence Perspective*. New York: Harper & Row.

Rhoades, G. & Sporn, B. (2002). New models of management and shifting modes and costs of production: Europe and the United States. *Tertiary Education and Management*, 8(1), 3-28.

Senge, P. M. (2000). Die Hochschule als lernende Gemeinschaft. In S. Laske & T. Scheytt & C. Meister-Scheytt & C. O. Scharmer (eds.), *Universität im 21. Jahrhundert: Zur Interdependenz von Begriff und Organisation der Wissenschaft* (pp. 509). München: Rainer Hampp.

Slaughter, S. & Leslie, L. L. (1997). *Academic Capitalism: Politics, Policies, and the Entrepreneurial University*. Baltimore: The Johns Hopkins University Press.

Sporn, B. (1995). *Adaptive University Structures: An Analysis and Comparison of U.S. and European Universities in Adapting to the Current Socioeconomic Environment* (Paper Presented at the Annual Conference). Orlando: ASHE.

Sporn, B. (1999). *Adaptive University Structures: An Analysis of Adaptation to Socioeconomic Environments of US and European Universities*. London: Jessica Kingsley.

Stensaker, B. (2000). Quality as Discourse: An Analysis of External Audit Reports in Sweden 1995–1998. *Tertiary Education and Management*, 6(4), 305-317.

Trow, M. (1973). Problems in the Transition from Elite to Mass Higher Education. In OECD (Ed.), *Policies for Higher Education* (pp. 51-101). Paris: OECD.

Weick, K. E. (1976). Educational Organizations as Loosely Coupled Systems. *Administrative Science Quarterly*, 21, 1-19.

BARBARA M. KEHM

INTERNATIONALISATION IN HIGHER EDUCATION:

FROM REGIONAL TO GLOBAL

Abstract. The contribution starts with a clarification of terms and concepts which have determined debates about internationalisation in higher education for the last few years. In particular, a differentiation is made between Europeanisation, internationalisation and globalisation. Then the main research approaches dealing with internationalisation in higher education are summarised in a typology from which the question is derived whether we are confronted with a trend towards harmonisation or further differentiation of institutional types and national systems due to internationalisation processes. Historically four phases of internationalisation in higher education can be distinguished with possibly a fifth phase currently starting and extending the perspective of internationalisation into that of globalisation. Higher education reforms between internationalisation and globalisation are then characterised by three main processes – a de-monopolisation of public higher education, a de-institutionalisation of studies and learning, and a de-nationalisation of policy – which lead to four areas of change. Internationalisation and currently globalisation act as catalysts for these changes. In a concluding chapter issues for further research and policy decisions are sketched on the micro, meso and macro levels.

INTRODUCTION

Issues of internationalisation have been an inherent part of EAIR since its very beginnings. Not only was the European branch of the American Association for Institutional Research (AIR) hatched and supported into life by the International Activities Committee of the latter organisation, it was set up with the intention to learn from each other and cooperate with each other. Transnational exchange of views and experiences as well as research results were prime reasons for getting EAIR started.

As internationalisation processes within higher education are characterised by considerable dynamics, the foci of discussing this theme have changed over the years. Still, in one way or another, internationalisation has been a topic of practically every Annual Forum of EAIR. This contribution will start with an analysis and clarification of terminology. It will then classify the main research approaches in the field, followed by a short historical account of policy changes. A further part will sketch four fields of higher education reforms which have been carried out or are currently being carried out in the context of higher education. Three ongoing processes result from these changes and reforms. In a concluding part, issues for further research with a strong interest to policy-makers are outlined.

DEFINITION OF TERMS AND CONCEPTS

Despite the strong rejection of the concept of globalisation in higher education by many leaders of European higher education institutions until quite recently, it has become an important issue in the last few years. EAIR's perspective and outreach has also become more global during the last decade or more attractive to participants in its Annual Forum from an ever increasing range of countries. But when the concept of

R. Begg (ed.), The Dialogue between Higher Education Research and Practice, 109–119.

globalisation entered the European higher education arena, many institutional leaders felt that internationalisation was the response of higher education to economic globalisation and that there was quite a difference between these two. Universities in particular felt that internationalisation and with it the free exchange of ideas and people had always been, and still was, an inherent feature of science and scholarship since the foundation of such institutions of higher learning. In contrast, globalisation was assumed to be about competition rather than cooperation, about making money rather than free exchanges. Also the European support programmes in the field of higher education like ERASMUS and now SOCRATES were established on the basis of principles such as mutual trust, cooperation and free flows of students and teachers. In short, globalisation was considered to be an unfitting, even 'dirty' word to characterise the aspirations of higher education institution and their leaders. Not any more! Today, more and more university leaders as well as policy makers in the field are aiming at turning their institutions into 'global players'.

On the national level of many European countries as well, a number of higher education reforms have been implemented during the last decade or – in some countries – are still in the process of being implemented; these are based on the argument that they are necessary in order to improve competitiveness of individual institutions and national systems as a whole, in the face of globalisation. So what does internationalisation actually mean in higher education and for higher education? Is it something in between Europeanisation on the one hand and globalisation on the other on a continuum that reaches from the regional to the global? Or are there different qualities and philosophies attached to the concept?

Internationalisation in higher education requires definition on two levels. First, internationalisation must be distinguished from Europeanisation on the one hand and from globalisation on the other. Second, the areas or levels must be determined in which processes of internationalisation are taking place in higher education. I shall rely here on some more or less heuristic definitions which have emerged in various reform debates about internationalisation in higher education. They serve to illustrate the different underlying philosophies.

- Europeanisation is seen as 'internationalisation light', as a space which is characterized by a common and shared history and culture, and finally as an economic, political and cultural alliance vis-à-vis the rest of the world, i.e. 'Europe as a fortress' (Teichler 2002: 8).
- Internationalisation reflects a world order which continues to be characterised by national states but leading increasingly to transnational and strategic relationships of exchange and cooperation (Scott 1998: 126).
- Globalisation, finally, reflects an emerging world order in which the borders of nation states and national steering are beginning to play a less important role, or even to erode, and in which processes of global competition start to dominate. The concept of globalisation is also linked with the emergence of the knowledge society which trades increasingly with immaterial goods like symbols, brand names, images and technological know-how. (Scott 1998: 127).

Thus, internationalisation is wider than Europeanisation but not as wide as globalisation; because borders continue to exist and with these also inclusions and exclusions. In addition, aspects of exchange and cooperation dominate in internationalisation while aspects of competition are more in the foreground of globalisation. In the face of internationalisation and globalisation, Europeanisation then can characterised as a specific form of 'regionalism'. If we look at institutional strategies in higher education, we find all three orientations: Europeanisation, internationalisation and globalisation.

But the argument is not just about spatial typologies. We also need to take into account the effects of Europeanisation, internationalisation, and globalisation on the structures, processes, tasks, and societal missions and visions of higher education institutions and systems. In the following line of argument internationalisation processes are used as a basic starting point while keeping in mind at the same time that the transition to a focus on European interaction on the one hand and a global interaction on the other are rather fluid. Processes of internationalisation in higher education can be identified on at least four levels.

a) We find efforts to internationalise degree programmes and teaching which are aiming to change the substance or the core (Teichler 2002) of what is being taught and studied and thus go beyond exchange and mobility. The intention is to strengthen intercultural competences in students as well as trans- and inter-disciplinary approaches in teaching and learning. Furthermore, aspects of quality development play an increasing role on this level.

b) We note efforts to create internationally transparent and compatible structures – think of what is being called the 'Bologna Process' – like the introduction of Bachelor and Master degrees, recognition and accreditation, credit point systems and modularisation. The goals related to these efforts are, for example, to assure international competitiveness of Europe as a whole, through comparability in the face of growing diversification, so that barriers for foreign students are reduced.

c) We note organisational reforms within higher education institutions replacing the traditional collegial model of governance by a more managerial approach. Not all these organisational changes have a direct relationship to processes of internationalisation but they are introduced or have been introduced with the argument to strengthen the central level so that institutions can become more strategic actors in the international or even global field. Goals are, for example, to increase institutional competitiveness and performance in national and international arenas, to increase innovative capacity as well as efficiency and effectiveness.

d) Finally, we clearly note an internationalisation of higher education policy and politics. Next to political actors on the national level and a larger autonomy of the institutional level, we see new actors, in particular international and supra-national organisations like the European Union, the OECD, the World Bank and UNESCO, trying to influence reform processes in and steering of higher education by promoting their own definitions of the functions and goals of higher education and by providing a variety of incentives.

These differentiations of the contextual frameworks in which internationalisation of higher education is discussed and taking place might suffice here in order to determine a high degree of complexity of the field. Add to that the aspects of internationalisation and globalisation of research.

MAIN RESEARCH APPROACHES

The number of publications in the field of internationalisation in higher education has grown so much during the last decade or so that it is impossible to provide an overview claiming to be somewhere near complete. However, among the attempts to deal with the topic we can distinguish six basic approaches which provide a typology:

1) Conceptual clarifications aiming at terminological definitions and a differentiation of analytical levels (e.g. Teichler 1998; 2000; 2002; Knight 1999; Scott 1998);
2) Critical assessment of dominating topics in the debates about internationalisation of higher education and related reform approaches and strategies (e.g. Teichler 2002; Kampf 2002);
3) State of the art reports and systematic overviews (e.g. Wächter et al. 1999; Gibbons 1998);
4) Studies and analyses of specific aspects of internationalisation, like mobility, new forms of degrees, recognition, quality issues, internationalisation of teaching and learning, institutional strategies (e.g. the ERASMUS studies of the Kassel Centre 1987ff.; Blumenthal et al. 1996; Schwarz & Teichler 2000; Van der Wende 1996; Barblan et al. 1998; Kehm 1998; 1999; 2001; Sporn 1999; Pellert 1999);
5) Studies about the internationalisation of national systems of higher education and international comparisons (e.g. Goedegebuure et al. 1993; Meek et al. 1998; Kälvemark & Van der Wende 1997; Campbell & Van der Wende 2000; Ollikainen 1999; De Wit 2001; Enders 2001);
6) Analyses of policies and programmes of international and supra-national organisations in the field of higher education (e.g. Haug et al. 1999; Van der Wende 1999; Gibbons 1998).

Although this is only a rather small scale attempt to provide a systematic overview of research approaches in the field, which has not taken into account the innumerable number of institutional case studies, we can see that the complexity of the field mentioned above is reflected in rather heterogeneous forms to approach it. However, it is interesting to note that recently an increasing number of attempts have been made to analyse the topic of internationalisation and globalisation in higher education from a systematic and classificatory perspective and that the reasons and motives for internationalisation, the framework conditions and activities and finally the institutional, national and supra-national policies are coming more strongly into focus.

One question has frequently come up in many of the research approaches and thematic foci listed here, the answer to which has so far been controversial: Do we have to expect a trend towards harmonisation or even convergence of higher education institutions and national systems of higher education – at least in Europe – or do current developments rather point to further differentiation and diversification of institutional types and national systems? An answer to this question will be attempted at the end of this contribution.

A BIT OF HISTORY

It has always been argued that an international outlook and perspective is one of the characteristic features of science and scholarship and an inherent trait of higher education. Pointing to the continuity of this trait from the wandering scholars of the Middle Ages until today's mobility of students, however, is not sufficient to explain our feeling that higher education and higher education institutions have become more international than before and that specific dynamics have been at work to put this into effect. The feeling of an increased degree of internationalisation in higher education can also not be explained in a quantitative way. Globally there have always been about two per cent of mobile students and that proportion has not changed over the years. So we need to find other reasons for our impression. Looking back historically there have always been thrusts of internationalisation in higher education accompanied by processes of deregulation and varying political motives. For Western Europe, Baron (1993; 1996) has distinguished four phases of internationalisation between 1950 and the end of the 1990s.

1) Between 1950 and 1975 internationalisation in higher education was mainly linked to mobility of students and researchers. It was predominantly a part of foreign policy and limited to a small number of mainly highly developed receiver countries, the USA being the most prestigious one. Germany in particular, followed a 'policy of open doors' for foreign students to improve its international reputation after World War II.

2) Between 1975 and 1987 a second phase started in which a more regulative and differentiated approach substituted the previous 'free mover' mobility. Study abroad of one's own students tended to be regarded as more important than receiving foreign students. In a number of European countries considerable financial means were provided from the national governments to reduce barriers to mobility. The first programmes were established to provide framework for organised mobility of students. Study abroad was considered an important educational experience. At the same time, the dominant patterns of mobility flows changed from the traditional South-to-North mobility to a growing North-to-North mobility.

3) The third phase, between 1987 and 1992, was characterised by the emergence of a new actor in the arena of mobility: the European Commission. In 1987, the ERASMUS Programme was established and quickly became the most successful mobility programme in Europe. Recently the one millionth student received financial support in order to study abroad for a few months within the framework of the Programme.

4) After 1992, with the Treaty of Maastricht and the European Commission's 'Memorandum on Higher Education', a fourth phase started. It was characterised, in particular, by a professionalisation of the structures which had been set up within higher education institutions to organise and support mobility of students and teachers (e.g. International Relations Offices). But other factors became notable as well. More and more higher education institutions themselves became independent and strategic actors in the processes of internationalisation. At the same time the European Commission was able to gradually strengthen its role as an important political actor in the

field of internationalisation of education as a whole. Other supra-national organisations, like the World Bank and the UNESCO, developed their own programmes and activities in the field and the countries of Central and Eastern Europe were slowly integrated into the relevant processes of internationalisation. So the European higher education space expanded.

During the last few years we can note the beginning of yet another phase in which questions of the market and competitive advantages – at the level of institutions as well as at the level of national systems of higher education – are moving slowly and not undisputedly into the foreground. The age of globalisation has started turning higher education from a public good into a marketable service, adding competition to cooperation, and re-interpreting exchange and mobility in terms of long-term economic investment, brain drain and brain gain. The new round of negotiations within the framework of the General Agreement of Trades in Services (GATS) has put globalisation on the political agenda in the field of higher education.

HIGHER EDUCATION REFORMS IN THE CONTEXT OF INTERNATIONALISATION AND GLOBALISATION

Internationalisation and even more so globalisation in higher education is triggering and accelerating national deregulations and reforms in an international rather than national perspective. Kampf (2002) has distilled three main processes:
1) A 'de-monopolisation' of public higher education through a growing provision of private higher education, higher education institutions established by companies, virtual provisions, branch campuses of foreign institutions, educational export franchising arrangements, etc.
2) A 'de-institutionalisation' of studies and learning through e-learning and online provisions, recognition of competences and qualifications gained informally and outside of higher education institutions, etc.
3) A 'de-nationalisation' of higher education policy through new and mostly international or supra-national actors, other arenas of negotiation and loss of national instruments of steering and governance.

Four areas of change will now be analysed in some more detail which accompany current efforts for further internationalisation and lead to the deregulations listed above. It can be said that internationalisation has a catalyst function for reform activities in the four areas.

(1)   Knowledge related changes: Internationalisation and even more so globalization has led to changes in the traditional forms of knowledge production, transmission and certification. With the new forms of knowledge production I am referring to the distinction between 'mode 1' (traditional form) and 'mode 2' (new form) as introduced by Gibbons et al. (1994) and Nowotny et al. (2001). New forms of knowledge transmission are related to the increasing use of information and communication technologies (e-learning, virtual provision, internet, etc.). And new forms of knowledge certification are related to various forms of recognition of qualifications, skills and experiential knowledge which has been acquired in informal ways, outside higher education or at higher education institutions abroad. We also find

a growing importance of knowledge which is not based on academic disciplines, and we are confronted with new definitions in terms of relevant knowledge (cf. Gibbons 1998). All these aspects affect the traditional structure and organisation of curricula. Furthermore, academic knowledge is increasingly dispersed over a variety of institutional frames. We have franchising operations, virtual provisions, branch campuses abroad, new types of private institutions or public-private partnerships. These developments are changing our traditional understanding of what constitutes discipline-based academic knowledge. Borders are eroding and knowledge is contextualised in new ways (cf. OECD 1998) threatening the function of the university, changing forms of validation, and confronting contemplative with performative knowledge.

(2)   Changes related to the concept of education: We note changes in the traditional understanding of what constitutes an education, in particular a higher education, and the functions ascribed to it. With this I am referring to the traditional, humanist liberal ideal of educating the character or the personality which loses its influence in favour of emphasising skills and international employability. This goes hand in hand with a loss of meaning of what Lord Dahrendorf (1965) termed 'education as a citizen's right' which is based on the view of education as a public good in favour of an increased importance of education as a service, a commodity and a market which is based on the view of education as a consumer good and students as customers.

(3)   Institutional changes: We note changes in institutional strategies starting with the erosion of the participative collegial model of governance in favour of new public management approaches. Institutional governance based on managerial models include new forms of systematic and internationally or globally oriented marketing and profile building at regional, national, international and global levels. Higher education institutions are becoming autonomous actors pursuing strategic goals and giving themselves a 'corporate identity'. Innovation, entrepreneurship, performance and competitiveness are elements of a trend towards further differentiation and diversification while at the same time there are attempts to create more transparency and compatibility.

(4)   Systemic changes: Finally, we note changes of the political arena into which higher education is embedded due to a growing number of corporative and non-governmental, international and supra-national actors. The existence and activities of these new actors affect the relationship between higher education and the state and change traditional forms and instruments of national steering of higher education. Representatives of various societal sectors, i.e. stakeholders, are becoming members of Boards of Governors, international accreditation and benchmarking is carried out including experts from professional organisations. Furthermore, we see the influence of the Bologna Process and the policies of OECD, UNESCO and – in the Central and Eastern European countries at least – the World Bank. The developments show a trend towards including new actors in the higher education policy arena with the effect that this arena becomes more hybrid and requires new forms of negotiation, debate and legitimation.

Despite the catalyst function of internationalisation for these four areas of change, it is necessary to state that the impact and importance of internationalisation varies for individual subjects or disciplines, for individual institutions, and for individual national systems of higher education. Already in 1990, Clark Kerr has pointed out the field of tension which exists between the trend to internationalise higher learning and the trend to nationalise the purposes of higher education (Kerr 1990). A similar characterisation of this development can be found in Teichler (2002) who spoke about the 'internationality of substance versus the nationality of form' and in Scott (1998). Most higher education institutions today assume a regional or national mission as well as an international or global one.

In the view of the institutions of higher education internationalisation serves to secure resources, to function as an element of quality assurance, and to increase reputation. Due to these functions, internationalisation becomes increasingly an object of strategic action which means that it has to be managed institutionally, it has a policy component, and it is an element of profile building, i.e. of external perception. In many European countries this has not only led to an increase of steering agencies and agents but also of the levels on which steering and regulations takes place. In consequence we can frequently note the paradoxical attempt to regulate deregulation, to force higher education institutions to become more entrepreneurial while at the same time attempts are being made to tame the market.

CONCLUSIONS AND ISSUES FOR FURTHER RESEARCH

In concluding this contribution I want to sketch a few issues for further research which will be relevant for policy makers as well. In the future, the dialogue between research, policy and practice that EAIR has been fostering during the last 25 years will have to include representatives, experts and professionals from the various new arenas of higher education professions, e.g. evaluators, middle level management, consultants, etc., but also from higher education steering and governance that internationalisation has been opening up. An indication of these new groups of actors will be given in the three issues for further research which are all placed at an intersection where research, policy and practice interact.

(1)   Coordination at the macro level: The famous 'Clark triangle' (cf. Clark 1983) of coordination between the state, the market and the academic oligarchy needs to be extended into a hexagon reflecting the increased number of relationships and interactions (see below).

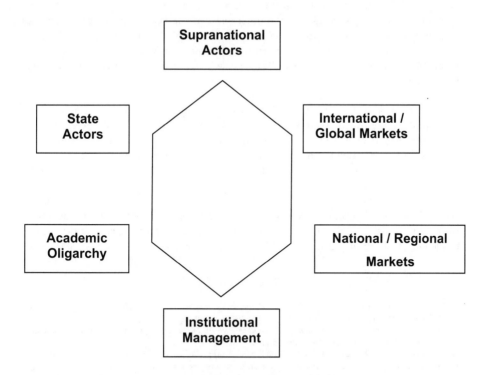

Figure 1. Hexagon of coordination.

Due to the multiplication of actors involved coordination and steering of higher education have clearly become more complex. In addition, societal demands directed towards higher education institutions in terms of their education and research performance have diversified. Further differentiation of systems within Europe on the one hand tends to be counterbalanced on the other by attempts – in particular by the Bologna Process - to create more transparency and compatibility. The question of whether we are heading towards growing convergence and harmonisation or towards increasing differentiation is not a simple either/or. It is both. In the face of increasing differentiation and diversification of institutions as well as national systems, policy makers are trying to develop mechanisms which enable continued mobility and comparative assessment and recognition.

Within the relationships and interactions indicated by the hexagon, higher education institutions have to position themselves today and in the future and have to shape their teaching and research accordingly. The introduction of internationally and even globally oriented elements of market and competition has led to a growing importance for each national system of higher education reform processes of other countries and of higher education policies of supra-national organisations. More research is needed about the contradictions and problems inherent in the new mix of steering and coordination.

(2)   Relationship between higher education and the state at the meso level: Within the existing relationship between higher education and the state a new definition of the

appropriate balance between state regulation on the one hand and institutional autonomy and self-governance on the other will become necessary. For policy analysis and research an interesting question will be: What will happen if higher education institutions and supra-national actors form an alliance and wrest further competences from the weakening state level? Will the market win or a new supra-national bureaucracy?

(3)   Institutional mechanisms of governance at the micro level: It continues to be an empirically unproven assumption that the new types of institutional governance, i.e. the new managerial approaches, will indeed be able to increase performance, innovative capacity, entrepreneurship, and competitiveness of higher education institutions on a larger scale. The new forms of regulation which have been implemented or are in the process of being implemented within the framework of new governance concepts still have to demonstrate their relative advantage over the traditional and more inclusive collegial models. Comparative research of the implementation processes and outcomes of these reforms, as well as guidelines on how to manage increasing complexity, will be challenging tasks in this field.

REFERENCES

Barblan, A. et al. (eds.) (1998). *Emerging European Policy Profiles of Higher Education Institutions*. Kassel: Wissenschaftliches Zentrum für Berufs- und Hochschulforschung.
Barblan, A. et al. (1999). *Implementing European Policies in Higher Education Institutions*. Kassel: Wissenschaftliches Zentrum für Berufs- und Hochschulforschung.
Baron, B. (1993). The Politics of Academic Mobility in Western Europe. *Higher Education Policy*, 6(3), 50-54.
Baron, B. (1996). International Education in European Universities: Where are we? Where do we go? Presentation at the *EAIE Conference*, December in Budapest (mimeo).
Blumenthal, P. et al. (eds.) (1996). *Academic Mobility in a Changing World*. London: Jessica Kingsley.
Campbell, C. & Van der Wende, M. (2000). *International Initiatives and Trends in Quality Assurance for European Higher Education. Brussels*: ENQA.
Clark, B. R. (1983). The *Higher Education System. Academic Organization in Cross-National Perspective*. Berkeley: University of California Press.
Dahrendorf, R. (1965). *Bildung ist Bürgerrecht. Plädoyer für eine active Bildungspolitik*, Bramsche/Osnabrück: Nannen-Verlag.
Enders, J. (2001). *Academic Staff in Europe: Changing Contexts and Conditions*. Westport (Conn.), London: Greenwood Press.
Gibbons, M. et al. (1994). *The New Production of Knowledge*. London: Sage.
Gibbons, M. (1998). *Higher Education Relevance in the 21st Century*. Washington: The World Bank.
Goedegebuure, L. & Van Vught, F. (eds.) (1994). *Comparative Policy Studies in Higher Education*. Utrecht: Lemma.
Haug, G. et al. (1999). Trends in Learning Structures in Higher Education. Project Report prepared for the *Bologna Conference on 18-19 June 1999*. Copenhagen: Danish Rectors' Conference.
Kälvemark, T. & Van der Wende, M. (2000). *National Policies for the Internationalisation of Higher Education in Europe*. Stockholm : National Agency for Higher Education.
Kampf, K. (2002). *Die Internationalisierung der deutschen Hochschulen. Dissertation*, Thesis submitted at Mainz University.
Kehm, B. M. (1998). Verpasste Internationalisierung? , *Zeitschrift für Kulturaustausch*, 48(1), 56-62.
Kehm, B. M. (1999). Strategic Management of Internationalisation Processes. Problems and Options. *Tertiary Education and Management*, 5(4), 369-382.
Kehm, B. M.; Pasternack P. (2001). *Hochschulentwicklung als Komplexitätsproblem. Fallstudien des Wandels*. Weinheim, Basel: Beltz.
Kerr, C. (1990). The Internationalization of Learning and the Nationalization of the Purposes of Higher Education: Two Laws of Motion in Conclict?, *European Journal of Education*, 25(1), 5-22.
Knight, J. (1999). Internationalisation in Higher Education.. In: Knight, J., De Wit, Hans (eds.). *Quality and Internationalisation in Higher Education* (pp. 13-28). Paris: OECD/IMHE.

Meek, L. V. et al. (eds.) (1998). *The Mockers and Mocked: Comparative Perspectives on Differentiation, Convergence and Diversity in Higher Education*. Oxford: Pergamon/IAU Press

Nowotny, H. et al. (2001). *Re-Thinking Science. Knowledge and the Public in an Age of Uncertainty*. Oxford: Blackwell.

OECD (1998). *Redefining Tertiary Education*. Paris: OECD.

Ollikainen, A. (1999). *The Single Market für Education and National Educational Policy*. Ph.D. Thesis, Turku: Turku University.

Pellert, A. (1999). *Die Universität als Organisation. Die Kunst, Experten zu managen*. Wien, Köln, Graz: Böhlau.

Schwarz, S. & Teichler, U. (eds.) (2000). *Credits an deutschen Hochschulen. Kleine Einheiten – große Wirkung*. Neuwied, Kriftel: Luchterhand.

Scott, P. (ed.) (1998). *The Globalization of Higher Education*. Buckingahm: SRHE and Open University Press.

Sporn, B. (1999). *Adaptive University Structures*. London: Jessica Kingsley.

Teichler, U. (1998). The Role of the European Union in the Internationlization of Higher Education. In: Scott, P. (ed.). *The Globalization of Higher Education*. Buckingham: SRHE and Open University Press, pp. 88-99.

Teichler, U. (2000). Internationalisierung als Aufgabe der Hochschule in Europa. In: Joerden, J. C. et al. (eds.). *Universitäten im 21. Jahrhundert*. Heidelberg: Springer, pp. 169-183.

Teichler, U. (2002). Internationalisierung der Hochschulen. In: *Das Hochschulwesen*, Vol. 50, No. 1, pp. 3-9.

Van der Wende, M. (1996). Internationalising the Curriculum in Higher Education. In: OECD (ed.). *Internationalisation of Higher Education*. Paris: OECD, pp. 35-89.

Van der Wende, M. (1999). The Bologna Declaration: Enhancing Transparency and Competitiveness of European Higher Education. Paper presented at the *Fourth Annual Conference of GATE*, Melbourne/Australia (mimeo).

Wächter, B. (ed.) (1999). *Internationalisation in Higher Education*. Bonn: Lemmens.

De Wit, H. (2001). *Internationalisation of Higher Education in the United States of America and Europe: A Historical, Comparative and Conceptual Analysis*. Ph.D. Thesis, Amsterdam: University of Amsterdam.

JOSE-GINES MORA AND LUIS E. VILA

THE ECONOMICS OF HIGHER EDUCATION

Abstract. This chapter synthesises what economists have learned about a number of key topics related to the provision of higher education and its roles in promoting economic development and well-being. The shift towards a global economy, as well as other economic changes brought about by technological and institutional development, have raised new concerns about the importance of post-secondary education in the enhancement of individuals and in the advancement of society as a whole. Economists translate these concerns into research questions of two main types. The first one includes questions about the production process within higher education institutions, that is, the mechanisms through which the resources allocated to higher education are transformed into educational outputs demanded by society. The second type of questions is about the relationships between the outcomes of higher education and people's well-being. The topics analysed cover both the private market and non-market returns to the investment in higher education, as well as the contribution of higher education to economic growth and to advances in equity.

INTRODUCTION

Economics is the study of how individuals and society decide to use resources, which are scarce and limited, to produce diverse goods and services, and the distribution of these goods and services among individuals and groups to fulfil the whole panoply of human needs. Therefore, the Economics of Higher Education is the study of the allocations of resources to the production of post-secondary educational services, the distribution of these services, and its effects among the population. Since the resources have alternative uses, education has to compete for resources with many other needs and wishes of people. Economics of Education, and consequently Economics of Higher Education, is a relatively recent field. Although classic economists had considered education, the development came in the second part of the 20th century, coincidentally with the tremendous expansion of education during that half century when, from a global perspective, education has shifted from a phenomenon of a social elite to a massive system with enormous consequences for economic life of individuals and societies. Since the concept of human capital was established in 1959 by Theodore Schultz, the Economics of Education has been a growing field, with theoretical contributions from many of the greatest economists of recent decades.

Both assignative and distributive issues have attracted the interest of researchers although most often they have been treated separately, leading to two main lines of research with little connection. Assignative issues include questions about the production process within higher education institutions, that is, the mechanisms through which the resources allocated to higher education are transformed into educational outputs demanded by society. Demand for education, financing, management of institutions, grants and human resources are some of the topics that are usually considered in this area. Distributive issues relate in general to questions about the relationships between the outcomes of higher education and people's well-being. The topics analysed cover both the private market and non-market returns on the investment in higher education, as well as its social returns in terms of its contribution to economic growth and to advances in equity and well-being.

R. Begg (ed.), The Dialogue between Higher Education Research and Practice, 121–134.

In addition to traditional approaches, some present trends currently influencing higher education practice, management and policy are:

- The shift towards a globalised economy.
- Shifts in where policy-making takes place: there is a shift upwards, from national to supranational level, and at the same time there is a shift downwards, from national to regional level.
- Science and technology policies: trends to integrating the contribution of the natural sciences - development of production technology - with that of the social sciences - development of social institutions - to expand general well-being.

This chapter synthesises what economists have learned about some of the key topics related to the roles of higher education in promoting economic development. We have selected only some of the most relevant aspects of the Economics of Higher Education. The rest of the chapter is organised as follows. The next section briefly analyses the traditional goals of higher education and the new challenges brought about by recent institutional and technological development. The third section deals with one of the most relevant aspects in the production process of higher education: the financing of higher education. The effects of higher education on well-being both of individuals and society are presented in the final section.

THE TRADITIONAL GOALS OF HIGHER EDUCATION

To disentangle the complex contribution of higher education to the development of societies and their economies, an understanding of the multiplicity of purposes simultaneously addressed by higher education institutions to meet social demands is needed. Broadly speaking, higher education exists to serve a multiplicity of purposes related to the creation and the transmission of knowledge to improve reality. The traditional missions of higher education institutions are to teach students, to carry on research and to provide services to the community.

The 'teaching' role covers the diffusion of existing knowledge by providing students with opportunities for instruction in the liberal arts as well as in advanced vocational training. The teaching role of higher education institutions has been historically driven by two separate and often conflicting philosophical views: the so-called 'meritocratic' and 'egalitarian' principles. The meritocratic conception stresses the relevance of teaching the more able individuals from all social classes to achieve productive citizenship, economic security, and higher social status for themselves and their families. The egalitarian conception focuses on the assumed capacity of higher education to reduce inequalities among individuals and classes in the economic and social system. The conflict between these two conceptions is at the basis of the development and expansion of higher education systems. Institutions are permanently confronted with the dilemma of providing excellence versus providing opportunity. In most European countries, the second half of the 20th century has witnessed the transition from elite HE systems to post-secondary education for almost everyone who wants it. Higher education promotes benefits for the educated individual and for efficiency and equity in society as a whole; consequently, extending higher education to all who desired it was viewed as the key tactic in increasing economic growth and decreasing society's inequalities. However, achieving these goals is not independent of how and what it is taught and learned in higher education institutions. Therefore, the institutional organisation of higher education becomes a key element to understanding whether and how higher education fulfils its teaching goal by delivering a quality undergraduate educational product.

The research goals of higher education institutions include the creation and diffusion of both basic and applied new knowledge. The demand for knowledge is derived from the demand for technical change in the production of goods and services – addressed by the research in the natural sciences - and from a demand for institutional change and improvements in institutional performance – addressed by the research in the social sciences. The knowledge obtained through academic research offers an opportunity to reduce the costs of innovation both in production and in institutional change.

The 'community services' role is addressed by the efforts of higher education institutions to extend their potential beyond their training and research functions. The creation of new knowledge by means of research is not sufficient; knowledge must go into the hands of those who would eventually use it. Institutions meet this need by organising a variety of activities. These include extending technical knowledge to the private sector and to policy makers, providing public affairs education, verifying knowledge generated by the private sector, and providing feedback mechanisms, such as the evaluation of the value of new knowledge and the identification of new relevant problems.

There is a growing concern about some perceived trends towards a declining emphasis on teaching and neglect of undergraduate education, due to the encouragement of research as an alternative use of the faculty's time (Hearn 1992). There are economic reasons explaining these trends:

-   Faculty's salary, promotion and tenure systems show that research productivity is the prime determinant of individual rewards in higher education institutions
-   rewards for research grew, while those for teaching remain stationary
-   financial constrains of institutions

Additionally, organisational theorists and researchers have pointed out that two organisational elements are at the basis of the threat to the education of undergraduates. The consequences of these issues operate as difficulties in offering high quality undergraduate education. First, measuring faculty's performance in teaching is more controversial than measuring their performance in research. The difficulties in defining and quantifying teaching quality are great, since professors and teachers interact in many complex ways with the students to produce the educational output. Second, higher education institutions face multiple resource dependencies. In the competition for resources, institutions seek to protect their primary sources. For many institutions, 'prestige' is the primary source of business. Prestige, of course, would be gained through both teaching and research activities. However, while research funding is generally based on quality, teaching is most often funded by quantity. Therefore, institutions seek for prestige, which in turn would increase their total resources and, consequently, they tend to encourage and reward preferentially research activities and to pay less attention to teaching performance.

FINANCING HIGHER EDUCATION

In western countries the development of higher education is high and participation and accessibility have reached a reasonable level. Higher education has become a mass system (though not yet universal) which strongly influences the way it is financed. The objective of higher education financing policy should be to combine the financial sufficiency of the system and the improvement of efficiency with equity. Nevertheless, equity has two meanings: Equal opportunities of access to higher education for people from any social class, and a fair share of the cost of higher education among the beneficiaries of the service. Let us discuss these aspects in the European context.

The financing of higher education in a mass higher education system

Several factors explain the financing troubles of higher education generated by the shift to a mass system. The first is the growing cost of higher education. In the last decades, several factors have increased the financial needs of higher education:
a) The growing number of students entering higher education. In some European countries, the number of higher education students increased tenfold from the 1960's to the 1990s and the rates of participation in higher education are reaching percentages of around 40 to 50 % of the youth at the relevant age.
b) The lack of stronger differentiation in the goals and structure of higher education institutions in some European countries. The Humboldtian model of university has extended in many European countries as the only system to transmit knowledge and to produce highly skilled people. Recent processes of diversification should have decreased the cost of higher education, but the non-university sector of higher education, initially focused on shorter programmes, has increased the academic drift towards longer courses, and demands more and more research funds. The negative effect is the increasing cost and the presence of inefficiencies for the whole higher education system in many countries.
c) Progressive concern about the amount and quality of services that universities are offering. In most countries, universities are involved in processes of growth and improvement in the services offered to students and the community in general.
d) The increase in the cost of higher education is also a consequence of its peculiar production system. Higher education is an intensive user of highly skilled personnel, whose salaries should be competitive with the salaries of those with the same educational level and skills working in other sectors. In the competitive sector of the economy, technological changes are being introduced progressively in the production system. Consequently, productivity increases and salaries rise for highly skilled workers. Nevertheless, the production system in higher education uses the same basic technology as centuries ago (lectures, tutorials and so on). The productivity of the system does not improve substantially but the costs (basically wages) rise at the same pace as in other productive sectors (Levin 1991).

The second reason for the financial crisis of higher education is the general crisis of the welfare state as a consequence of the strong competition for public funds from different social services in modern states. Governments feel greater pressure from other sectors that have grown enormously in recent years. The reduction of public expenditure and the balancing of the budget are priorities in most countries.

Finally, another cause for the financial crisis is related to the changing role of higher education in modern states. A basic mission of universities in the last two centuries was to prepare the elite capable of steering the state. This is especially true in countries following the so called Napoleonic model of university. The state was inclined to finance higher education because universities were basically a service of the state that fulfilled its need for skilled people for the public service. Moreover, the size and consequently the cost of the higher education system, did not represent a great burden for the public budget. The extension of higher education that took place in the last decades in European countries changed the main role of higher education institutions, transforming them into institutions which are more focused on serving the needs of the productive system, and society in general. The state is not the main user of the higher education system anymore and, consequently, it is more reluctant to finance higher education on its own.

On the other hand, it is commonly agreed that economic growth and competitiveness, based on the progress of new knowledge is a serious challenge for economic growth. Thus, the current investment in higher education may not to be enough to sustain a sector, which is a key factor for future development. In Europe these ideas have been stressed in the last years (EC 1991) and specially in the recent document 'The role of the universities in the Europe of knowledge' (EC 2003).

In summary, nowadays there is a profound contradictory situation: the need for a well-financed higher education system and the incapacity of the states to finance the whole bill. How do we solve this situation? Generally speaking, economists support the idea of increasing private financing of higher education. As we shall discuss in the next pages, there are important economic reasons that support the fairness of a greater private share in the financing of higher education.

Public vs. private funding

The trend towards a greater contribution of private funds to the financing of higher education is based upon economic rationale and the belief that the market is the place where economic production becomes more efficient and effective. Nevertheless, as has been discussed extensively in the economic literature, the market is not a perfect representation of higher education and you cannot rely exclusively on it to finance higher education (Leslie & Johnson 1974). This is why higher education is, to a greater or lesser extent, financed through public funds in all countries.

The public contribution to the cost of higher education rests on arguments of both efficiency and equity. In terms of efficiency, higher education generates external benefits not captured in the form of higher earnings or additional non-pecuniary benefits by the person who has received higher education. Among these benefits, we can point to the ability of individuals with higher education to raise the productivity of those they work with, that is, the increase in the productivity of the fellow workers to adapt to technological change, and to introduce innovation. When society as a whole receives benefits from higher education, some of the cost should be paid by public funds.

On the other hand, imperfection and uncertainty in the higher education market also explain the public intervention on grounds of efficiency. Higher education is costly, the monetary benefits or future earnings are uncertain because of dropout of students and the difficulties that graduates have in finding employment. Without public support, students would have to borrow heavily to finance their studies and demand would be below the economic optimum. In brief, public funding of higher education is continued because markets cannot provide the socially optimum quantities and quality of education, as markets do not capture externalities.

Equity reasons are based on the principle that higher education should be available to people with capacity, disregarding their economic resources, in order to increase the fairness in society. It would be impossible to reach this goal through market mechanisms. In consequence, the state should implement policies to equalise opportunities of access to higher education. There are two basic mechanisms for reaching this objective: lowering tuition fees below the real cost of instruction in public institutions, or setting up programmes of grants and/or loans to aid people from lower socio-economic backgrounds. The first policy (low fees) subsidises everybody attending higher education institutions, without regard to their economic backgrounds; the second could be more specifically for people in need.

On the other hand, a higher education degree has a high value in the labour market for individuals. In OECD countries, unemployment for university graduates is considerably lower than the average, and the salaries are remarkably greater for higher education graduates, compared with people with lower educational levels (OECD 2002).

Although the percentage of higher education graduates in the labour market has increased remarkably in the last decades in Europe, the position in the labour market of graduates remains at a reasonably good level (Teichler & Kehm 1995; Mora et al. 2003). In Spain, for instance, during the 1980s, the number of higher education graduates in the labour market shifted from eight hundred and fifty thousand to over one and half million. In spite of this remarkable increase, the high earnings differential of those graduates related to basic levels of education did not change (Vila & Mora 1998). This result shows the higher uptake of higher education graduates by the labour market, though there are some difficulties in the transition from the educational system to the labour market.

Labour market benefits are only a part of the benefits that individuals with a higher education degree obtain. Other economic and social benefits are more difficult to quantify, but there is general agreement that graduates not only have more employability and receive higher earnings, but also acquire higher social status, greater efficiency in consumption, better health, greater access to technological change and a broad set of cultural benefits including better opportunities for leisure.

Benefits from education are also gained by enterprises. General education reduces the need for training and retraining when new technologies are incorporated. The higher productivity of more educated people, especially those having the abilities and skills that transmit higher education, is spilled out to other workers - having an important effect on the whole productivity of the enterprise. A considerable part of the externalities that higher education graduates produce is captured not only by society in general (which justifies the public funding of higher education), but specifically by enterprises. On the other hand, enterprises are the primary and more direct beneficiaries of the scientific and technical advancement produced largely in universities. Consequently, the participation of enterprises in the funding of higher education institutions, through research contracts, provision of services and philanthropic funds, could be considered as a consistent restitution for the benefits that corporations receive from higher education.

In conclusion, it is clear from an economic point of view that private benefits, for individuals and enterprises, are very high. There is also a consensus that social benefits are substantial, though less measurable (Eicher & Chevaillier 1993). In consequence, the principle of who benefits must pay leads to a mixed system of private and public financing of higher education. A problem remains unsolved: what should be the division of public and private funding? Economics does not give us an exact answer to this question, but it could be stated that the current proportion in most European countries is unfair from the point of view of equity in the sources of the funds and, in addition, generates expensive inefficiencies.

A better balance between public and private funding of higher education should be the consequence of:
a) The recognition that the benefits of higher education accrue to private individuals and their employers.
b) The expectation that competition for funds will increase institutional efficiency and responsiveness to economic and social needs.
c) The recognition that social equity would improve if, at the same time, a rational system of student aids is developed (Taylor 1991).

The increased private participation in higher education financing could be implemented in several ways:
a) Establishing basic tuition fees that represent a substantial part of instructional costs.
b) Establishing specific fees for special services.
c) Developing business contributions to finance continuing education and training.
d) Possibility of introducing earmarked taxes on corporations for education (Eicher & Chevaillier 1993).

The increasing of the tuition fees is a key aspect in this mode towards a better balance between public and private financing. For equity reasons, there is full agreement that an increase of privatisation of higher education through tuition fees must be accompanied by a substantial growth in student aid. To avoid the risk of implementing a policy of increasing tuition but at the same time not an equivalent policy of student aid, an automatic link between both policies should be established. Comparative studies of these policies in different states of the United States show that some equity problems have arisen when the two policies are not linked (Griswold & Marine 1996).

A general trend is also to decrease the parental and taxpayer's share of the financing for higher education and to increase the share borne by students through loans. These loans should be guaranteed by the state and should include an income threshold to be achieved before repayments become due, though another alternative is to make monetary contributions for repayment of loans dependent on lifetime income (Woodhall 1992). The introduction of a scheme of loans would introduce co-responsibility in the sharing of the cost and could help in improving efficiency, at least in countries where the real duration of studies is too long due to students taking a long time in finishing their studies (Oosterbeek 1998).

Finally, we would like to remark that what is true in more developed countries, where higher education has reached high levels of accessibility, is not necessarily true in other countries at a lower stage of development of higher education. In these countries, a stronger public participation could be important in order to promote higher education and to guarantee equity for people from a lower social background. Although some experts (World Bank 1994) recommend a partial privatisation of higher education in developing countries, others argue, "the first best method of funding higher education in developing countries is out of general tax revenues by the state. However, when governments are unwilling to finance higher education due to socio-economic and political pressures, including international pressures, second best solutions have to be found" (Tilak 1997: 19).

THE OUTCOMES OF HIGHER EDUCATION AND PEOPLE'S WELLBEING

Higher education as personal investment

Monetary returns

The time and money invested in education does pay returns, and these returns have a positive net effect on the opportunities for satisfaction of human needs. The benefits of education may be realised in terms of increased production possibilities and reduced need to incur costs. The benefits that directly increase production possibilities or reduce costs are relatively easy to conceptualise and measure, since they can be addressed in monetary terms by looking at the corresponding markets. Under the human capital approach, extensive research has been conducted on the identification and measurement of monetary returns on schooling. Most economic analysis on the value of education has focused on the contribution of formal schooling to increased earning capacity in the labour market. Longer schooling improves the chances of employment (Rivera-Batiz 1992; Iyigun & Owen 1999), reduces the duration of unemployment (Kiefer 1985; Kettunen 1997) and positively influences income through higher labour market earnings. The estimation of monetary returns on education has generated a vast amount of empirical literature, which has been reviewed, among others, by Psacharopoulos (1996) and Cohn and Addison (1998). Such overviews, however, need to be examined with care since estimates are often not directly comparable because of differences on sample coverage and on methodology. Card's (1999; 2001) studies on the causal relationship between education and earnings through the analysis of the main econometric problems in the recent literature leads to four key conclusions. First, ordinary least square (OLS) estimates of returns contain some upward ability bias of about 10%. Second, studies on twins do reduce this ability bias. Third, the ability bias on estimates that use instrumental variables are in general higher than those corresponding to OLS estimates. Fourth, school quality and parental education do positively influence the rate of return on education. In the light of these conclusions, the most reliable estimates of rates of return to education would come from studies on samples of twins, like those in Ashenfelter and Rouse (1998), Ashenfelter and Krueger (1994) and Miller et al. (1995).

Non monetary returns

Studies on rates of return only estimate part of the effects of education because the economic benefits that higher education bestows are not limited to higher expected production or lower production costs. The benefits could also consist of direct additions to welfare possibilities. Part of the benefits of higher education that improve well-being directly are likely to be reflected in higher income, and hence captured by rates of return analysis, but it is clear that traditional pecuniary measures do not capture all the utility-enhancing effects of education. The non-monetary benefits of education (NMB) may be defined as those educational outcomes for which the full economic impacts escape pecuniary measurement. Extensive enumeration and discussion of the evidence on NMBs may be found, among others, in Michael (1982), Haveman and Wolfe (1984), McMahon (1998) and Vila (2000).

To date, two main approaches are found in the literature on the NMBs of education. First, a number of studies focus on those benefits that accrue to the person being educated, and to other identifiable beneficiaries, from individual investment in schooling. Sander (1999), Nayga (1998), Grossman and Kaestner (1997), Kenkel (1991) and Berger and Leigh (1989) are examples of studies providing evidence on the effects of higher education on health status. Discussion and some evidence on the links between education and fertility can be found, among other, in Klepinger et al. (1998), Brien and Lillard (1994), Rosenzweig and Schultz (1989) and Psacharoupoulos and Woodhall (1985). Evidence of the effects of parents' education on children's health, cognitive development and social behaviour can be found, among others, in Leigh (1998), Grogger (1997), Angrist and Lavy (1996), Kaestner and Corman (1995) and Wolfe and Behrman (1982). Some evidence on benefits related to occupational and consumption choices, including improved household management, is also available, although the effects confirmed by research are only a part of those identified. Under the second approach, the attention focuses on those effects promoting well-being for all the population at the same time. Improved education to more inclusive social groups has been positively linked to economic growth and development. Besides, education helps to increase social cohesion, and to reduce income inequality, although complementary conditions may be required.

An approach to total returns

From a general perspective, Arrow (1997) suggested that longer schooling promotes a more efficient use of information both on the formation of expectations and on individual choices regarding the labour market. Therefore, better-educated people are thought to both form more accurate expectations and pursue their aspirations more efficiently than poorly educated people. As a consequence, highly educated individuals are likely to reap additional education-enhanced benefits in terms of personal utility arising from better-matched preferences on non-pecuniary aspects of their working activity.

The analysis of job satisfaction may help to simultaneously shed light on both monetary and non-monetary effects of education investment on people's well-being. Self-assessments of job satisfaction indicate how workers value the whole package of both pecuniary and non-pecuniary returns from their jobs according to their own personal preferences and expectations. Therefore, job satisfaction may be used to gain insight into the effects of workers' education on total utility from work and, ultimately, on general welfare. Survey responses on job satisfaction have been used in economic analysis as proxy data for utility from work, with job satisfaction being in turn a key determinant of total well-being for working individuals. This approach has been econometrically validated (Van Praag 1991) leading to a rapidly increasing body of literature on the economics of happiness (for an overview, see Veenhoven 1996).

Most of the discussion has focused on the effects of observable job/individual attributes such as wages, firm size, trade union membership, age, race and gender (see, among others, Sloane & Williams 1996; Watson et al. 1996; Hamermesh 2001; Blanchflower & Oswald 2002). The evidence on the effects of education level on job satisfaction is, however, rather inconclusive: some papers report neutral or negative influences (see, for example, Idson 1990; Clark 1996; Clark & Oswald 1996) while the results from others imply positive effects (see, among other, Meng 1990; Hartog & Oosterbeek 1998). There are two main reasons that explain these mixed results. The first reason is that most analyses do not include any other education-related variables, apart from schooling level or length as a determinant of job satisfaction. However, workers' perceptions about the match between their education and their current jobs are likely to influence self-assessments of job satisfaction. The results reported by Hersch (1991), Johnson and Johnson (2000), and Belfield and Harris (2002) are supportive of this proposition. The second reason is that most studies focus on overall job satisfaction and place little emphasis on the study of the effects of education on workers' satisfaction with specific dimensions of work. Nevertheless, the effects of education on satisfaction across diverse aspects of the job may be heterogeneous, and there may be significant education-related differences in the weights different individuals put on satisfaction from different aspects of work. The analysis conducted by Groot and Maasen van den Brink (1999) lends empirical support to these ideas. They conclude that the influences of individual/job characteristics on job satisfaction do differ according to the aspect of the job considered, and that the response to a question on overall job satisfaction does differ from responses to questions on satisfaction with particular aspects of the job. Therefore, analysis of the effects of worker's education on satisfaction with specific aspects of work is called for in order to learn more about the total effects of education investments on utility from work-related sources.

Higher education as social investment: economic growth

During the last two decades, and particularly in the 1990s, the levels of GDP per capita diverged not only between the US and the EU, but also across EU countries and often across regions within some countries. These disparities are explained because of the fact that some economies, either at national or at regional level, were able both to increase the number of people working and improve their productivity, while others were not.

According to OECD (2000) the relationship between science, technology and economic performance appears to have changed in the 1990s. Innovation is now considered more critical to success in business and, ultimately, to the growth of economies. Information and communication technologies (ICT) play a capital role in facilitating innovation though the diffusion of technological and organisational developments. Technology and innovation are the main drivers of increased economic growth performance in developed countries. Moreover, productivity gains, understood as increases in multi-factor productivity (MFP), are mainly the result of the application of new technology along with more efficient ways of organising production. In this changing environment, the role of education in explaining divergences in economic growth among countries and regions becomes capital. The education of the labour force is at the root of both technological and organisational developments; moreover, the diffusion of innovation in through ICT's also relates to the availability of a sufficiently educated workforce (Scarpetta et al. 2000). Early empirical work by Denison (1961) proposed an analysis of education based on a growth accounting framework, using an aggregate production function where the output Y depends on the stocks of capital K and labour L. His estimates showed that around 23% of the rate growth in US output, between 1930 and 1960, is explained by the increased level of education of the workforce. Nadiri (1972) used the same approach on a sample of developing economies, with mixed results for the rate of output growth explained by education (4.1% for Colombia; 23.2% for Ghana).

The relationship between education and economic development at the macro-economic level was initially studied within the framework of growth theory models developed by Solow (1956). Lucas (1988) extended the neo-classical growth model by considering human capital as a proxy for the utilisation of knowledge. In Lucas' approach, workers choose what fraction of time to devote to production and what to human capital accumulation. Workers' competences can be enhanced by the accumulation of human capital through education. Total output is a function of the number of workers and of the level of human capital competences. The model allows the distinction between internal and external effects of human capital accumulation on economic growth. The internal effect is the direct effect of the acquisition of human capital competences on total productivity. The external effect arises from an increased average level of human capital competences in the economy. In fact, as Doyle and Weale (1994) pointed out, two external effects may be distinguished. First, a higher average level of competences in the economy raises individual productivity. Second, the investment in human capital constantly raises the level of competences, which may be understood as a longitudinal externality. Consequently, the human capital theory should be integrated with the economic growth theory to include both the internal and external effects of the investment in education.

Aghion and Howitt (1992) considered economic growth fostered through the innovation driven by research. Van Marrewijk et al. (1992) explicitly considered three production inputs: physical capital, labour and human capital. These analysis differ from that of Lucas in that human capital is seen as a third factor of production instead of an element enhancing the effective labour supply. Mankiw et al. (1992) used school attendance as a proxy for human capital to estimate a production function where technical change is assumed to be exogenous. Under this approach, increases in the stock of human capital translate directly into economic growth through a higher elasticity than that corresponding to the other production resources. Differences in growth rates across regions and/or countries are then explained by differences in human capital competences emerging from differences in the educational attainment of the workforce.

Romer (1990) expanded the framework by considering an economy where new knowledge generates a positive external influence through learning-by-doing effects. Consumption goods are produced as a function of the stock of knowledge and of other inputs. Within this framework, the output per capita can grow without bounds, the rate of investment and the rate of return to capital may increase with the capital stock. Education would influence economic growth also indirectly through its impact over the generation and assimilation of technical innovations. Technology is generated through the investment in R&D activities which, in turn, require intensive use of highly educated labour. As a consequence, higher education influences economic growth not only directly, but also indirectly through the generation and the assimilation of new technology. It is clear, however, that improving growth performance depends on the combination of many factors and policies with higher education playing a key role.

REFERENCES

Aghion, P. & Howitt, P. (1992). A Model of Growth through Creative Destruction. *Econometrica*, 60, 323-351

Angrist, J.D. & Lavy, V. (1996). *The Effect of Teen Childbearing and Single Parenthood on Childhood Disabilities and Progress in School.* National Bureau of Economic Research Working Paper 5807. Washington: NBER.

Arrow, K. (1997). The Benefits of Education and the Formation of Preferences. In J.R. Behrman and N. Stacy (eds.): *The Social Benefits of Education.* Ann Arbor: University Of Michigan Press.

Ashenfelter, O. & Krueger, A.B. (1994). Estimates of the Economic Return to Schooling from a New Sample of Twins. *American Economic Review* 84(5), 157-1173.

Ashenfelter, O. & Rouse, C.E. (1998). Income, Schooling, And Ability: Evidence from a New Sample of Twins. *Quarterly Journal of Economics* 113, 253-284.

Belfield, C.R. & Harris, R.D.G. (2002). How Well Do Theories Of Job Matching Explain Variation In Job Satisfaction Across Education Levels? Evidence For U.K. Graduates. *Applied Economics*, 34(5), 535-548.

Berger, M. & Leigh, J.P. (1989). Schooling, Self-Selection and Health. *Journal of Human Resources*, 24(3), 433-455.

Blanchflower, D.G. & Oswald, A.J. (2002). *Well-Being Over Time In Britain and The USA.* National Bureau of Economic Research Working Paper 7487. Washington: NBER.

Brien, M.J. and Lillard, L.A. (2001). Education, Marriage and First Conception in Malaysia. *Journal of Human Resources*, 29(4), 1168-1204.

Card, D. (2001). Estimating the Return to Schooling: Progress on Some Persistent Econometric Problems. *Econometrica*, 69(5), 1127-1160.

Card, D. (1999). The Causal Effect of Education on Earnings. In: O. Ashenfelter & D. Card (eds.) *Handbook of Labor Economics, Volume 3.* Amsterdam: Elsevier Science

Clark, A.E. (1996). Job Satisfaction in Britain. *British Journal of Industrial Relations*, 34(2), 189-217.

Clark, A.E. & Oswald, A.J. (1996). Satisfaction and Comparison Income. *Journal of Public Economics*, 61(6), 359-381.

Cohn, E., & Addison, J.T. (1998). The Economic Returns To Lifelong Learning In OECD Countries. *Education Economics*, 6(3), 253-307

Denison, E.F. (1961). *The Sources of Economic Growth in the United States.* New York: Committee for Economic Development.

Doyle, C. & Weale, M. (1994). Education, Externalities, Fertility and Economic Growth. *Education Economics*, 2(2), 129-167.

EC (1991). *Memorandum on Higher Education in the European Community*, Brussels, Commission of the European Communities.

EC (2003). *The role of the universities in the Europe of knowledge*, Brussels, Commission of the European Communities.

Eicher, J. C. & Chevaillier, T. (1993). Rethinking the finance of post-compulsory education. *International Journal of Educational Research*, 19, 445-519.

Griswold, C. P. & Marine, G. M. (1996). Political Influences on State Policy: Higher Tuition, Higher Aid, and the Real World, *The Review of Higher Education*, 19(4), 361-389,.

Grogger, J. (1997). Local Violence and Educational Attainment. *Journal of Human Resources*, 32(4), 659-681.

Groot, W. & Maasen van den Brink, H. (1999). Job Satisfaction of Older Workers. *International Journal of Manpower*, 20(5/6), 343-360.

Grossman, M. & Kaestner, R. (1997), Effects of Education on Health. In: J.R. Behrman and N. Stacy (eds.): *The Social Benefits of Education.* Ann Arbor: University of Michigan Press.

Hamermesh, D.S. (2001). The Changing Distribution of Job Satisfaction. *Journal of Human Resources*, 16(1), 1-30.

Hartog, J. & Oosterbeek, H. (1998). Health, Wealth and Happiness. Why Pursue A Higher Education? *Economics of Education Review*, 17(3), 245-256.

Haveman, R. H. & Wolfe, B.L. (1984). Schooling and Economic Well-Being: The Role of Nonmarket Effects. *Journal of Human Resources*, 19(3), 378-407

Hearn, J.C. (1992). The teaching role of contemporary American Higher Education: Popular Imagery and Organizational Reality. In: W.E. Becker and D.R. Lewis (eds.) *The Economics of American Higher Education.* Boston, Dordrecht, London: Kluwer Academic Publishers.

Hersch, J. (1990). Education Match and Job Match. *Review of Economics and Statistics*, 73, 140-144.

Idson, T.L.(1990). Establishment Size, Job Satisfaction and the Structure of Work. *Applied Economics*, 22, 1007-1018.

Iyigun, M.F. & Owen, A.L. (1999). Entrepreneurs, Professionals and Growth. *Journal of Economic Growth*, 4, 213-232.

Johnson, G.J. & Johnson, W.R. (2002). Perceived Overqualification and Dimensions of Job Satisfaction: A Longitudinal Analysis. *Journal of Psychology*, 134(5), 537-555.

Kaestner, R. & Corman, H. (1995). *The Impact of Child Health and Family Inputs on Child Cognitive Development*. National Bureau of Economic Research Working Paper 5257. Washington: NBER.

Kenkel, D.S.(1991). Healthy Behaviour, Health Knowledge, and Schooling. *Journal of Political Economy*, 99(2), 287-305

Kettunen, J. (1997). Education and Unemployment Duration. *Economics of Education Review*, 16(2), 163-170

Kiefer, N. (1985). Evidence on the Role of Education on Labor. *Journal of Human Resources*, 20(3), 445-452

Klepinger, D., Lundberg, S. and Plotnick, P. (1999). How Does Adolescent Fertility Affect the Human Capital and Wages of Young Women? *Journal of Human Resources*, 34(3), 422-448

Leigh, J. P. (1998), Parents' Schooling and The Correlation Between Education and Failtry. *Economics of Education Review*, 17(3), 349-357

Leslie, L. L. & Johnson, G. P. (1993). The market Model and Higher Education. *Journal of Higher Education*, 45(1). 1974. (Reprinted in Breneman, D. et al (ed.) (1993), *ASHE Reader on Finance in Higher Education*, Needham Heights, Mass., Simon and Schuster Custom Pub.

Levin, H. M. (1991). Raising Productivity in Higher Education. *Journal of Higher Education*, 62(3), 137-158.

Lucas, R.E. Jr. (1992). On the Mechanics of Development. *Journal of Monetary Economics*, 22, 3-42.

Mankiw, G., Romer, D. and Weil, D. (1992). A Contribution to the Empirics of Economic Growth. *Quarterly Journal of Economics*, 107, 407-438.

McMahon, W. (1998). Conceptual Framework for the Analysis of the Social Benefits of Lifelong Learning. *Education Economics*, 6(3), 309-346.

Meng, R. (1990). The Relationship Between Unions and Job Satisfaction. *Applied Economics*, 22, 1635-1648.

Michael, R.T. (1982). Measuring Non-Monetary Benefits of Education: A Survey. In: W. McMahon and T. Geske (eds), *Financing Education: Overcoming Inefficiency And Inequity*. Urbana: University of Illinois Press.

Miller, P., C. Mulvey & Martin, N. (1995). What Do Twins Studies Reveal About the Economic Returns to Education? A Comparison of Australian and U.S. Findings. *American Economic Review*, 85(3) 586-99.

Mora, J.G., García-Montalvo, J. & García-Aracil, A. (2003), The Employment Situation About Four Years After Graduation. In: U. Teichler (Ed.), *Comparative Perspectives on Higher Education and Graduate Employment and Work – Experiences from Twelve Countries*. Dordrecht: Kluwer Academic Publishers. (Forthcoming).

Nadiri, M.I. (1972). International Studies of Total Factor Productivity: A Brief Survey. *Review of Income and Wealth*, 18,129-154.

Nayga, R.M. (1998). A Note on Schooling and Smoking: The Issue Revisited. *Education Economics*, 7(3), 253-258.

OECD. (2000). *A New Economy? The Changing Role of Innovation and Information Technology in Growth*. OECD: Paris.

OECD. (2002). *Education at a Glance*. OECD: Paris.

Oosterbeek, H. (1998). An Economic Analysis of Student Financial Aid Schemes. *European Journal of Education*, 33(1), 21-30.

Psacharopoulos, G. (1996). Returns to Investment in Education: A Global Update. *World Development*, 22(9), 1325-1343.

Psacharoupoulos, G. & Woodhall, M. (1985). *Education For Development: An Analysis of Investment Choices*. Oxford: The World Bank/Oxford University Press.

Rivera-Batiz, F.L. (1992). Quantitative Literacy and the Likelihood of Employment among Young Adults in the United States. *Journal of Human Resources*, 27(2), 318-328.

Romer, P.M. (1990). Endogenous Technical Change. *Journal of Political Economy*, 98, 71-102.

Rosenzweig, M.R. & Schultz, T.P. (1989). Schooling, Information, and Nonmarket Productivity: Contraceptive Use and its Effectiveness. *International Economic Review*, 30(2), 457-477.

Sander, W. (1999). Cognitive Ability, Schooling and the Demand for Alcohol by Young Adults. *Education Economics*, 7(1), 53-66

Scarpetta, S., Bassanini, A., Pilat, D. & Schreyer P. (2000). *Economic Growth in the OECD Area: Recent Trends at the Aggregate and Sectoral Levels*. OECD Economics Department Working Papers. OECD: Paris.

Sloane, P.J. & Williams, H. (1996). Are Overpaid Workers Really Unhappy? A Test of the Theory of Cognitive Dissonance. *Labour*, 10, 3-15.

Solow, R. (1956). A Contribution to the Theory of Economic Growth. *Quarterly Journal of Economics*, 70, 65-94.

Taylor, M. G. (1991). New Financial Models. *Higher Education Management*, 3(3), 203-213.

Teichler U. & Kehm, B. (1995). Towards a New Understanding of the Relationships between Higher Education and Employment. *European Journal of Education*, 30(2), 115-132.

Tilak, J. B.G. (1997). The Dilemma of Reforms in Financing Higher Education in India. *Higher Education Policy*, 10(1), 7-21.

Van Marrewijk, C., De Vries, C.G. & Withagen, C. (1992). Optimal Localised Production Experience and Schooling. *International Economic Review*, 33, 91-110

Van Praag, B.M.S. (1991). Ordinal and Cardinal Utility. An Integration of the Two Dimensions of the Welfare Concept. *Journal of Econometrics*, 50, 69-89.

Veenhoven, R. (1996). Developments in Satisfaction Research. *Social Indicators Research*, 37, 1-46.

Vila, L.E. & Mora, J. G. (1998). Changing Returns to Education in Spain during the 1980's. *Economics of Education Review*, 17(2), 173-178.

Vila, L. E. (2000). The Non-Monetary Benefits of Education. *European Journal of Education*, 35(1), 21-32.

Watson, R., Storey, D., Wynarczyk, P. Keasey, K. & Short, H. (1996). The Relationship Between Job Satisfaction and Managerial Remuneration in Small and Medium-Sized Enterprises: An Empirical Test of Comparison Income and Equity Theory Hypotheses. *Applied Economics*, 28, 567-576

Weisbrod, B.A. (1964). *External Benefits of Education*. Princeton: Princeton University Press, Industrial Relations Section.

Wolfe, B. L. & Zuvekas, S. (1997). Nonmarket Outcomes of Schooling. *International Journal of Education Research*, 27, 491-502.

Wolfe, B. L. & Behrman, J.R. (1982). Determinants of Child Mortality, Health, and Nutrition in a Developing Country. *Journal of Development Economics*, 11(10), 163-194.

Woodhall, M. (1992). Changing Sources and Patterns of Finance for Higher Education: A Review of International Trends. *Higher Education in Europe*, XVII(1), 141-149.

World Bank. (1994). *Higher Education: The Lessons of Experience. Development in Practice*. Washington: World Bank.

FRANS KAISER AND JEROEN HUISMAN

EXPANSION AND DIVERSIFICATION IN HIGHER EDUCATION

Abstract. Given the growth of national higher education systems, questions of access, expansion and diversification have regularly been addressed by higher education policy-makers and researchers. Often a straightforward relationship is presumed between the growth of the student body and the expansion of higher education systems and between the growth of the student numbers and diversification of such systems. This chapter presents an alternative approach to these phenomena. A theoretical model is built around the concept of 'carrying capacity'. The preliminary empirical findings – using data from the Netherlands and Australia – support the assumed role of, for example, national GDP, labour force productivity and the number of higher education graduates in explaining total enrolments in higher education. The findings regarding the relationship between enrolments and diversity were not in line with the expectations. The alternative approach, nevertheless, seems worth pursuing.

INTRODUCTION

Expansion of higher education systems is ubiquitous. The growing student body in the 1960s and 1970s has lead to the establishment of new higher education institutions, be it new universities or new types of institutions (*Fachhochschulen*, polytechnics, *hogescholen*, etc.). Policy-makers thought that setting up new organisations and, consequently, new study programmes was necessary to cope with the sheer quantitative growth as well as an assumed increasing variety of demands on higher education. Whereas this image particularly relates to Western Europe, similar patterns can – in more recent times – be noted in other parts of the world, such as Central and Eastern Europe. In systems where the most impressive growth has been some decades ago, expansion is continuing at a different pace, but also in different ways. Whereas previously most expansion took place in the public higher sector, nowadays private sectors or individual private organisations enter the scene. Whereas once the full-time mode prevailed for the traditional age group, nowadays part-time and distance education for traditional and non-traditional target groups is of significant magnitude.

The emerging pattern of 'more' and 'different' would easily lead to the conclusion that the growth of student numbers led to the expansion of the systems (for which specific government policies have been developed and implemented), in its turn leading to diversification of these systems. Diversification is here defined as the increase of (organisational) variety in a higher education system (see Huisman 1995). But also a co-evolutionary development of expansion and diversification can be assumed: expansion and diversification mutually reinforce each other. In general, the higher education literature assumes that expansion and diversification in higher education goes hand in hand, that there is a gradual monotonic increase of diversity over time, and that government policies have largely contributed to the pattern of expansion and diversification (see e.g. Trow 1974; Meek et al. 1996; Teichler 2002).

Nevertheless, there are theoretical reasons and empirical indications to suspect such expectations. Birnbaum (1983), for instance, found that in a period of unprecedented expansion (in terms of student numbers) of the US higher education system (1960–80), institutional diversity only increased marginally. This finding

R. Begg (ed.), The Dialogue between Higher Education Research and Practice, 135–145.

challenges the taken-for-granted relationship between expansion and diversification. In a different vein, Huisman et al. (2000; 2003) have analysed the relationship between participation and diversity in a number of Western European higher education systems and have analysed developments regarding participation, access and diversity through time in a number of these countries. They observed that growth in higher education enrolment is strongly related to growth patterns of gross domestic product (GDP). This lead them to the 'disturbing' conclusion that higher education policy related to the expanding higher education seems only of minor importance (if of any). In other words, expansion is driven by factors other than policy instruments. Teichler (2002) qualifies diversification in the process of expansion, by adding that structural patterns and policies come and go in cycles, which implies a much more dynamic interplay between expansion, government policies and diversification.

The challenge for this contribution is therefore to unravel the factors that impact expansion, with a particular focus on diversification in higher education. As such, our contribution is questioning the taken-for-granted impact of policies on the expansion and diversification of higher education systems. We propose an analytical model, based on economic and system theoretical approaches, and preliminary test – both quantitatively and qualitatively – to what extent this model holds.

The structure of the contribution is as follows. First, we explore the theoretical underpinnings and sketch a model regarding factors influencing expansion (or shrinkage) of higher education systems. We also present a model concerning factors influencing diversification (or homogenisation). Second, we use longitudinal data from Australia and the Netherlands to 'test' the feasibility of the models. Third, we reflect on the preliminary findings.

THEORETICAL CONSIDERATIONS REGARDING EXPANSION

Our point of departure is the concept of 'carrying capacity', rooted in ecology studies. This theoretical approach claims – regarding expansion – that organisational and system growth are limited by the environment's 'carrying capacity'. Carrying capacity is often equated with environmental resources (insured patients in a hospital, government funding for a service agency, manufacturing workers for an industrial union, customer purchases for a business - see Brittain 1994: 358). More generally, we should look at human, technological and financial sources that play a role in the system's environment. The theoretical approach therefore would expect that expansion of higher education is dependent on the carrying capacity allowing for growth.

Regarding participation, ecology studies would maintain that a population (of higher education students) will grow (mutatis mutandis) according to an S-shaped pattern (Verhulst-Pearl logistic equation). That is, a relatively sharp increase in the beginning and then a flattening of the growth towards the carrying capacity. If the population reaches the carrying capacity, a relatively stable situation emerges. Of course, the reality is more dynamic, because other populations grow and decrease as well, having an impact on the resources available, and consequently on the original population. In practice, therefore, the growth pattern will often deviate from the ideal-typical S-shaped form (see Pianka 1994: 182-187).

CARRYING CAPACITY IN HIGHER EDUCATION

In translating this concept into the realm of higher education from an economic and system's perspective, our starting point is supply-oriented. We state that the carrying capacity of a society is the amount of resources that society is willing or able to provide for the supply of higher education. This sets the upper limits to the expansion of the higher education system. For that willingness to provide those resources, a frequently used indicator is available: the total amount of resources (both from public and private sources) spent on higher education[1].

In addition to the supply-oriented approach we use a demand-oriented approach. Here, the growth of the higher education system is limited by the amount of higher education degree holders a society can absorb, as long as the structure of an economy remains the same (in terms of knowledge intensive industry and the absorption of technological change (Barth 2001). If the labour market is 'saturated' with higher education degree holders, their relative position on the labour market (in terms of salaries and employment chances) will deteriorate. And since we assume that students will enrol only if the perceived benefits of further higher education exceed its costs (see Becker 1992), such a drop in perceived benefits will lead to a decline in enrolment.

In order to identify the ways the supply- and demand-oriented approaches to carrying capacity in higher education relate to each other, the following argument is built. It starts with the straightforward supply orientation. A rise of the gross domestic product (GDP) of a country will lead to an increase in the amount of resources for higher education. Such an increase in the resources for higher education will be used to invest in higher education capacity. This capacity can be seen as student places available. Given a demand for higher education that exceeds the capacity, the increase in capacity will lead to an increase in the number of new entrants, adding to the level of enrolment (see Figure 1).

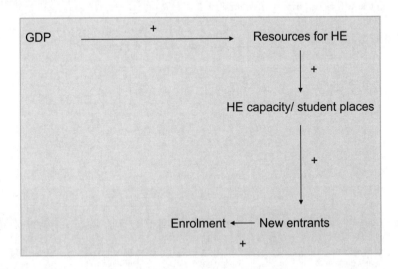

Figure 1. The relationship between GDP, resources and enrolments.

The assumption of excess demand is crucial in this argument: if the capacity exceeds the demand, other factors will determine the number of new entrants. This leads to the question how the demand for higher education is determined. The processes that affect the demand for higher education are a complex and broad set of economic, social, cultural and personal factors. We do not pretend to unravel this in this contribution. Our focus is mainly economical, the assumption being that the (growth rate of the) demand for higher education will diminish if potential students think their perceived direct costs will be outweighed by the perceived benefits of taking up a course in higher education. According to human capital theory, the individual choice to enrol is determined by the perceived benefits from his or her investment in prolonged higher education. The main benefits are the income premium and the low chances on unemployment. So, in addition to population size and eligibility criteria for access to higher education, relative wages and unemployment rates are major factors. Rises in both may tip the balance in favour of the benefits, which will lead to an increase in demand and enrolment (assuming that the capacity is greater than demand).

A significant decrease in the perceived benefits of a higher education study will lead to a decrease in demand and enrolment. This situation may occur if the supply of higher education degree holders to the labour market increases. Assuming that the demand for higher education degree holders is constant, an increase in supply will lead to a decrease of the wages or a rise of unemployment. Both will reduce the perceived benefits of a higher education study, which will have an effect on the continuation rate of secondary school leavers into higher education (see Figure 2).

The final step in drafting our model is to relax our assumption of a fixed economic structure and a fixed upper limit to the demand for higher educated workers. According to Barth (2001), the demand for higher educated workers is not fixed. For example, due to changes in the use and absorption of new technology and knowledge, the amount of higher education degree holders the labour market can absorb may increase, without lowering the wages or employment chances.

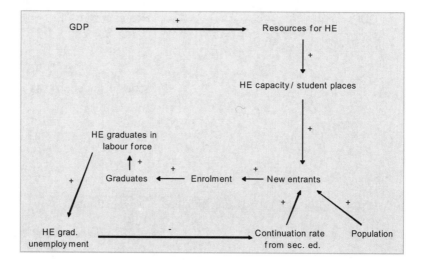

Figure 2. Introducing a negative feedback loop.

Now a second line of argument enters the model. It starts with the observation that two major determinants for the growth of GDP are labour force participation and the productivity of the active labour force. A higher labour participation and a higher productivity will lead to a growth of GDP. It is argued that both participation and productivity are influenced by the educational attainment of the population. A higher proportion of higher education degree holders in the population will lead to a higher participation rate and a higher productivity. In other words, if the proportion of higher education degree holders in the active labour force grows, GDP will grow.

Now the circle is closed, relating one aspect of the carrying capacity (the supply of higher education) to another (the demand for higher education degree holders). Figure 3 depicts the full argument. However, how strong the relations are and, even more important, what the effect of the time lags (which can be assumed to be considerable) might be in the interaction, has yet to be resolved.

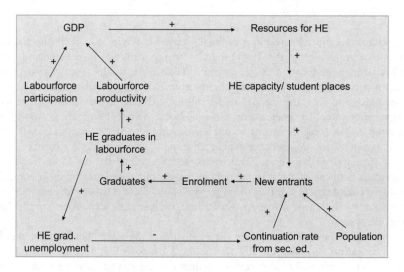

Figure 3. Closing the circle: higher educations output influences GDP.

CARRYING CAPACITY AND DIVERSIFICATION

Now we have drafted a 'simple' model in which the concepts of carrying capacity and expansion are related to each other, we need to bring in the concept of diversification. Can we relate diversification to the concept of carrying capacity and, by doing so, establish a link between expansion and diversification?

It seems – at least from an ecological perspective – difficult to directly connect diversity to the model already developed. Population ecology theory (Hannan & Freeman 1977: 944) states:

> ... the upper bound on [organizational] diversity is equal to the number of distinct resources plus the number of additional constraints on growth (Levin 1970) ... implies on the one hand that the change in constraint structure ought to lower organizational diversity through the elimination of some population.

In the traditional ecological models the idea of resource variety is most aptly illustrated by the impact of latitude (the closer to the tropics, the more diversity), altitude (the higher, the lower diversity), productivity (e.g. solar energy: the more productivity, the higher the diversity), size of the area (the larger, the more variety; this particular stems from research on islands) and spatial heterogeneity.

A line of reasoning coming close to the ecological perspective, can be found in Windolf's (1997) work. He has analysed the relation between differentiation and expansion[2]. He states that

> When the expansion attains the stage of mass education, counterforces are mobilized that either put a brake upon continued expansion or lead to a differentiation in the educational institutions. (Windolf 1997: 97).

In terms of carrying capacity, Windolf argues that this capacity of a system is expanded by institutional differentiation. Without institutional differentiation, a system will arrive at its carrying capacity and the growth of the higher education system will eventually decrease and halt.

But how can such a relationship be understood? Where does it fit into the model as it is drafted above? In the model there is no segmentation in the demand for and outflow of higher education degree holders. That is, the model assumes that potential students are indifferent regarding their choice of a particular higher education programme, and that the labour market absorbs degree holders, indifferent to the chosen programme. In other words, a degree holder may get any job, no matter what programme(s) he took. This is of course a gross and inaccurate simplification. There is segmentation in the demand for higher education degree holders, which calls for a diverse supply of higher education programmes. We argue that the more frequent the mismatches between demand and supply in the various segments, the more limited the carrying capacity gets (even if on the aggregated level there is no unmet demand). These limitations to the carrying capacity will limit the possible expansion of the higher education system.

Another possible limitation to the expansion is the match between the supply of higher education programmes and the demand by potential students. In the model drafted above, the body of potential students is conceived as a monolithic entity. However, it can be argued that the potential student body is diversified/segmented and that each segment has its own preferences in terms of higher education programmes.[3] The more frequent the mismatches between demand/potential students and the offering of programmes, the more limits there will be to the expansion of the higher education system.

We have not found references in the literature in which the segmentation approach is related to the process of diversification in higher education. Although the relationship has a high degree of plausibility, we have not succeeded in corroborating our line of reasoning with empirical results. Further empirical and conceptual work needs to be done in this promising line of research. That is why the arrows in Figure 4 are marked with question marks. In the following section on results, we shall return to the question of the relationship between expansion and diversification, although in a different way.

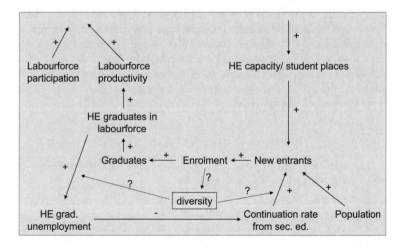

Figure 4. Ecological model including diversification.

As has been said, the objective here is not to determine the exact weights of the variables in the models, but to reconsider the relevance of the traditional, straightforward models that are so dominant in the higher education literature and in the minds of many (governmental) policy-makers. The models proposed differ in the elaboration of the recursive character of the key indicators (GDP, enrolment and diversification). On the one hand they may complicate the discussions because the introduction of the feedback loops blurs the difference between dependent and independent variables. On the other hand they may help to structure the discussions in a way that does a little more justice to the complex character of higher education systems. In the remainder of this contribution we look into the model a little further by using existing data on the relevant indicators for two higher education systems: the Dutch and the Australian.

METHODOLOGY

The relationships described in the model (Figure 3) are illustrated by empirical data for two higher education systems of similar size: the Netherlands and Australia. We present bivariate correlation coefficients (Pearson correlation) for the variables that are directly related in the model. GDP data originate from OECD. The resources for higher education refer to all sources of income of higher education institutions. We did not identify any direct measures of the higher education capacity. Data on new entrants, enrolment and graduates related to undergraduate programmes. The labour market related data were derived from labour force surveys. The period the data refer to differs by variable and country. Data on student flows, GDP and expenditure covered the longest period: from the 1970s until 2000. Labour market related data, especially those with a higher education reference spanned in the Netherlands the period 1990-2000, for Australia 1996-2000. Statistics are presented on student flows, labour force, unemployment, GDP and expenditure on higher education. For the Netherlands, the data span the period 1970-2001. For some indicators (labour force and unemployment statistics by educational attainment), the period covered is shorter: 1990-2001.

Regarding the relationship between expansion and diversification, following the 'model' proposed by Windolf, we would expect that the growth rate of enrolment is positively correlated to the diversity index. We used the enrolment data from the sources described above. With respect to diversity we calculated a diversity index much used in ecological studies and also applied in higher education studies (see Birnbaum 1983; Huisman et al. 2003). The higher the index (values range from '0' to '1'), the more diverse the higher education system.

RESULTS

In Table 1, we have listed the bivariate correlations between the variables that are, according to the model, related to each others.

Table 1. Bivariate correlations.

Variable 1	Variable 2	NL	Aus
HE resources	New entrants	**.95**	**.99**
New entrants	Enrolment	**.96**	**.99**
Enrolment	HE graduates	**.93**	**.99**
HE graduates	HE degree holders LF	**.79**	.94
HE degree holders in LF	LF productivity	**.96**	
Size of LF	GDP	**.97**	**.99**
LF productivity	GDP	**.98**	
GDP	HE resources	**.99**	**.97**
Unemployment benefit	New entrants	**-.76**	**-.96**
Proportion HE degree holders in LF	Unemployment benefit	-.47	**-.98**

Notes: Pearson correlation
         bold: significant at 0.05 level
         LF: labour force
         Unemployment benefit: rate of unemployment minus rate of unemployment
         among HE degree holders

Most of the variables are correlated to each other, which confirms the 'simple' logic of the model. In addition, the signs of the correlations are in line with the model. However, the correlations are all very high. This raises a serious suspicion that an underlying trend dominates the scores of the variables and causes the high correlations. A way around this problem would be to estimate the trends and focus on the residuals from those trends. However, the combination of this and the impact of substantial time lags we assume to be relevant in our model made this approach not feasible in the context of this contribution.

Regarding diversity, the data in Table 2 and Figure 5 suggest another pattern than suggested by the expectation. Diversity in Australia has decreased in the period under study, while enrolment has increased. In the Netherlands, diversity has remained stable, but enrolment has grown (but at a much slower pace than in Australia).

Table 2. Diversity scores and number of institutions for Australian and Dutch higher education (1980-1996).

| | Australia | | The Netherlands | |
	Diversity index	no. of institutions	Diversity index	no. of institutions
1980	.978	89	.964	360
1985	.973	64	.961	104
1990	.927	56	.963	95
1996	.798	36	.974	79

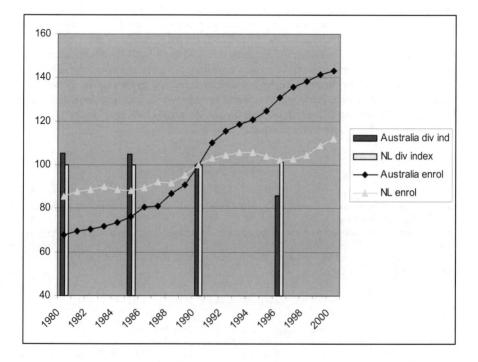

Figure 5. Changes in enrolment and diversity score in Australian and Dutch higher education. (1990=100)

DISCUSSION

Taking the ecological literature as a starting point for an analysis of the relationship between expansion and diversification requires a different type of approach than the one usually applied in higher education research. A caveat of the approach is that the complex and recursive modelling requires data that are not yet available to us. In addition, the model presented is not a comprehensive conceptual framework that may fully explain the developments in higher education expansion. The number of variables selected is small, which implies a massive reduction of complexity. Despite this, the model goes beyond the simple, straight-forward (mental) models that are used by some policy-makers. A first 'test' indicates that the data fit the model, although we warned for the neglect of including time-lags.

Diversification is seen, not only by policy-makers, as a crucial condition for further higher education expansion. In many national policy documents, diversity is the major instrument to enhance the carrying capacity of society for enrolment in higher education. Our results undermine this certainty.

There may be two explanations of this surprising result. The first one is that diversification is not a critical factor for the expansion of a higher education system. Other factors, possibly such as the ones identified in our model, have a much stronger impact on the expansion. If this were true, to be confirmed by studies including other countries, diversification policies may be fruitful, but not if the aim is to allow for (more) expansion. A second explanation continues along the line of reasoning in the ecological approach and focuses on the relationship between carrying capacity and the level of diversity. It may be the case that expansion rates have not yet reached the carrying capacity (see the section on theoretical considerations). This would imply that enrolment may still rise – even considerably – without a necessary increase of diversity. Also, even a decline of diversity might not directly harm the expansion of the system. Elaborating the conceptual frameworks based on ecology theory, and developing the data required for testing those frameworks, are the daunting challenges that lie ahead of us, exploring the links between expansion and diversification.

NOTES

[1] We assume that there are no restrictions on the availability of the main production factors, like (academic) staff, buildings and laboratories.

[2] Windolf uses the term 'differentiation', but in fact he refers to the same concept (diversification) as we have used.

[3] Furthermore it can be argued that the heterogeneity of the potential student body is enhanced by the process of expansion.

REFERENCES

Australian Bureau of Statistics (various years), *Education and Work*. Canberra: ABS.
Australian Bureau of Statistics (various years), *Transition from Education to Work*. Canberra: ABS.
Barth, E. & Roed, M. (2001). Do we need all that higher education? Evidence from 15 European Countries. In: *Public funding and private returns to education PURE*, www.etla.fi/PURE
Becker, W.E. (1992). Why go to college? The value of an investment in higher education. In: W.E. Becker & Lewis, D.R. (eds.), *The economics of American higher education*. Boston: Kluwer Academic Publishers.
Birnbaum (1983). *Maintaining diversity in higher education*. San Francisco: Jossey-Bass.
Brittain, J. (1994). Density-independent selection and community evolution. In: J.A.C.Baum & J.V.Singh (eds.), *Evolutionary dynamics of organizations*. New York: Oxford University Press.
Centraal Bureau voor de Statistiek (2003). Statline, www.cbs.nl
Centraal Bureau voor de Statistiek (1992). *Het onderwijs vanaf 1950*. Den Haag: CBS.
Centraal Bureau voor de Statistiek (various years). *Enquête Beroepsbevolking*. Den Haag: CBS.
Department of Education, Training and Youth Affairs (various years). *Finance, Selected Higher Education Statistics*. Canberra: DETYA.
Department of Education, Training and Youth Affairs (various years). *Selected Higher Education Student Statistics*. Canberra: DETYA.
Huisman, J. (1995). *Diversity, differentiation and dependency in higher education*. Utrecht: Lemma.
Huisman, J., Kaiser, F. & Vossensteyn, H. (2000). Floating foundations of higher education policy, *Higher Education Quarterly*, 54(3), 217-238.

Huisman, J., Kaiser, F. & Vossensteyn, H. (2003). The relations between access, diversity and participation: searching for the weakest link? In: M. Tight (ed.), *Access and exclusion*. Amsterdam etc: JAI Press.

Meek, V.L., Goedegebuure, L., Kivinen, O., Rinne, R. (eds.) (1996). *The mockers and mocked: comparative perspectives on differentiation, convergence an diversity in higher education*. Oxford: Pergamon Press.

Pianka, E.R. (1994). *Evolutionary ecology*. New York: Harper Collins College Publishers.

Teichler, U. (2002). Diversification of higher education and the profile of the individual institution, *Higher Education Management and Policy* 14(3), 177-188.

Trow, M. (1997). Problems in the transition from elite to mass higher education. In: OECD (ed.), *Policies for higher education*. Paris: OECD.

Windolf, P. (1997). *Expansion and structural change*. Boulder: WestviewPress.